Edited by

John McK. Camp II / Craig A. Mauzy

THE ATHENIAN AGORA

NEW PERSPECTIVES ON AN ANCIENT SITE

Zaberns Bildbände
zur Archäologie

Sonderbände der
ANTIKEN WELT

Published in collaboration with the

American School of Classical Studies at Athens

Edited by John McK. Camp II / Craig A. Mauzy

THE ATHENIAN AGORA

NEW PERSPECTIVES ON AN ANCIENT SITE

144 pages with 88 color and
75 b/w images.

Cover:

Hephaisteion (interfoto, München)

Page 2/3:

View from Hephaisteion (C. A. Mauzy,
American School of Classical Studies at Athens).

Back cover:

Painting, attributed to J. J. Wolfensberger, 1834
(see Fig. 88).

Reconstructed Stoa of Attalos
(see Fig. 23).

Stoa of Attalos Gutter Well pottery
(see Fig. 70).

www.zabern.de

Information of Deutsche Nationalbibliothek:
<http://dnb.d-nb.de>

Printed in Germany by Philipp von Zabern, on fade resistant and
archival quality paper (PH 7 neutral) · tcf

Layout:
Melanie Barth, scancomp GmbH, D-Wiesbaden

Coordination of production:
Ilka Schmidt, Verlag Philipp von Zabern, D-Mainz

Editorial department:
Alrun Schößler and Annette Nünnerich-Asmus,
Verlag Philipp von Zabern, D-Mainz

Table of Contents

Preface

The Agora of Athens was the center of the ancient city, a large, open square where the citizens could assemble for a wide variety of purposes. On any given day the space might be used for a market, an election, a dramatic performance, a religious procession, a military drill, or an athletic competition. Here administrative, political, judicial, commercial, social, cultural, and religious activities all found a place together in the heart of Athens, and the square was surrounded by the public buildings necessary to run the Athenian government.

These buildings, along with monuments and small objects, illustrate the important role played by the Agora in all aspects of public life. The council chamber, magistrates' offices, mint, and archives have all been uncovered, while the law courts are represented by the recovery of bronze ballots and a water clock used to time speeches. The use of the area as a marketplace is indicated by the numerous shops where potters, cobblers, bronze-workers, and sculptors made and sold their wares. Long stoas (colonnades) provided shaded walkways for those wishing to meet friends to discuss business, politics, or philosophy, while statues and commemorative inscriptions reminded citizens of former triumphs. A library and concert hall met cultural needs, and numerous small shrines and temples were sites of regular worship. Given the prominence of Athens throughout much of antiquity, the Agora provides one of the richest sources for our understanding of the Greek world in antiquity.

The Background to This Book

This volume originated in the celebrations of the 75th anniversary of the beginning of excavations by the American School of Classical Studies at Athens in the Athenian Agora, held in 2006. It is structured around two essays: the first, by John Camp, introduces the archaeological results and the second, by Craig Mauzy, presents a brief pictorial history of the excavations. Each introductory essay is followed by a series of short chapters. The first group comprises contributions in various fields of scholarship (architecture, sculpture, epigraphy, pottery, and amphoras), highlighting recent research in these areas at the Agora. The second group, contributed by excavation staff members, covers new advances in how the excavations are recorded and how new finds are treated (conservation, survey and drafting, record-keeping, and archives). The demands of a long-term excavation such as that of the Agora means that all who work there are part of a continuum stretching back to the digging of the first trench in 1931; others have worked on the project before and others will come after. This project — still in progress — has drawn on the talents and resources of hundreds of scholars and students who have worked together to enhance our understanding of Athens through the ages. It is hoped that this volume will serve to review the past, to indicate the present state of the work, and to suggest what may lie in the future.

In addition to the contributors to this volume, many other individuals have worked for the success of this project and it is appropriate to record and acknowledge their contributions here. The archives and offices have been under the competent and dedicated management of Jan Jordan and Sylvie Dumont for many years. Staff artist Annie Hooton has contributed to many Agora publications through her drawings, and photographer Angelique Sideris has provided numerous images. In recent years the conservation department has benefited from the work of Wendy Porter, Claudia Chemello, Amandina Anastassiades, and Karen Lovén. A large project to computerize the Agora archives has been under the supervision of Patricia Felch, ably assisted by Irini Marathaki, Pia Kvarstrom, Vasili Spanos, and Frederick Ley. George Dervos and Maria Stamatatou have handled numerous logistic duties.

Other papers on Agora topics were delivered in Athens during the 75th anniversary by John Hayes (Roman pottery), Maria Liston (bones), and Marianne Stern (glass) but have not been included here for reasons of space. A photo exhibit and illustrated volume on the history of the Agora excavations (*Agora Excavations 1931–2006: A Pictorial History*, Athens 2006) were prepared by Craig Mauzy. In addition, an exhibition and accompanying catalogue on the watercolors of Piet de Jong, curated by John Papadopoulos, were prepared by Agora staff and scholars (*The Art of Antiquity: Piet de Jong and the Athenian Agora,* Athens 2007).

The Agora Today

Also celebrated in 2006 was the 50th anniversary of the reconstruction of the Stoa of Attalos, completed in 1956, to serve as the site museum. Built originally by King Attalos II of Pergamon in ca. 150 B.C. as a gift to the Athenians, it served as a major commercial center until its destruction in A.D. 267. It now houses a display area and provides working space and storage for the excavations. On display in the public galleries is a selection of the thousands of objects recovered in the last 75 years, reflecting the use of the area from 3000 B.C. to A.D. 1500. Most significant, perhaps, is the material — unique to the site — illustrating the mechanics of the world's first attested democracy, such as ostraka (inscribed potsherds) used as ballots to exile overly ambitious politicians, allotment machines and bronze identification tags used in selecting Athenian juries, and tokens and inscribed lead strips used in the administration of the Athenian cavalry.

Context is essential in understanding archaeological material. The great museums of Europe and the United States often display magnificent objects with little or no information as to where they were found and what else was found with them. What sets the Agora project and museum apart from most collections is the relationship of the objects to the archives. Because the excavations began so late, a generation or more after other large-scale digs around the Aegean (Knossos, Delphi, Olympia, Pergamon, Ephesos, and Priene, to name a few), the same recordkeeping system adopted at the beginning has been used to the present day, supplemented of course by new technology. This means that every object found in the Agora excavations is stored in the Stoa of Attalos, a reconstructed Hellenistic building, together with the record of its recovery. The inventory is large: 35,000 pieces of pottery, 7,600 inscriptions, 3,500 pieces of sculpture, 5,000 architectural fragments, 6,000 lamps, 15,000 stamped amphora handles, and more than 70,000 inventoried coins. This vast collection has all been entered in a unified database, part of a collaborative project with the Packard Humanities Institute. Because of this correlation of objects and archives, the museum collection serves as a center for archaeological research, used by hundreds of scholars from all over the world.

Unlike the work of most European scholars, American archaeology in Greece is funded almost entirely by private funds, given by either foundations or individuals. In the early years, fieldwork at the Athenian Agora was funded by John D. Rockefeller Jr.; other support has come from the Samuel H. Kress, Andrew W. Mellon, Gladys Krieble Delmas, and Ford foundations as well as the European Union. The recent excavations have been made possible through the support and collaboration of the David and Lucile Packard Foundation and the Packard Humanities Institute. The Packard Humanities Institute has also undertaken the task of bringing the excavations into the digital age. It is fitting to record here our thanks to the Institute and its president, David W. Packard, for support essential to the continuation and success of the Agora excavations.

THE ARCHAEOLOGY OF
THE ATHENIAN AGORA

The Archaeology of the Agora: A Summary

by John McK. Camp II

The area of the Agora was first laid out as a public space in the 6th century B.C. Administrative buildings and small sanctuaries were built, and water was made available at a fountain house fed by an early aqueduct. Following the total destruction of Athens at the hands of the Persians in 480/79 B.C., the city was rebuilt and public buildings were added to the Agora one by one throughout the 5th and 4th centuries B.C., when Athens contended for hegemony over Greece. During this Classical period the Agora and its buildings were frequented by statesmen such as Themistokles, Perikles, and Demosthenes, by the poets Aeschylos, Sophokles, Euripides, and Aristophanes, by the writers Thucydides and Herodotos, by artists such as the sculptor Pheidias and the painter Polygnotos, and by philosophers such as Sokrates, Plato, and Aristotle. Together, they were responsible for creating a society and culture that set a standard against which subsequent human achievements have been judged. The Agora was the focal point of their varied activities and here the concept of democracy was first developed and practiced.

With the rise of Macedon under Philip II (382–336 B.C.) and Alexander the Great (356–323 B.C.), all significant military, economic, and political power shifted to the East during the subsequent Hellenistic period (3rd–2nd centuries B.C.). In the spheres of education and philosophy, however, Athens maintained its preeminence. The Academy, founded by Plato, and the Lyceum, founded by Aristotle, continued to flourish. They were supplemented by the arrival of Zeno of Kition (335–263 B.C.), who chose to lecture at the Agora in the Painted Stoa (also known as the Stoa Poikile). Athenian cultural dominance continued throughout the Roman peri-

od, and the buildings added to the Agora reflect the educational role of the city, a role which ended only with the closing of the pagan philosophical schools by the Christian emperor Justinian in A.D. 529. With the collapse of security in the empire, Athens and the Agora suffered from periodic invasions and destructions: the Herulians in the 3rd century A.D., the Visigoths in the 4th, the Vandals in the 5th, and the Slavs in the 6th. Following the Slavic invasion, the area of the Agora was largely abandoned and neglected for close to 300 years.

An anniversary is a good time to look back and consider what has been accomplished since the outset of the project. The story of the Agora excavations has been presented in many ways over the years, usually following a historical or topographical format. Because the Agora was a multifunctional, multidimensional place, however, it seems useful here to consider the results of the excavation thematically, to present what we know about different aspects of life in ancient Athens as a result of these long-term excavations.

When selecting themes we must, however, remember that functions were much more mingled in antiquity, when a running race, for example, might be classified both as an athletic event and as a religious occasion. Also, not surprisingly, the emphasis on the different uses of the Agora changed during the more than 750 years it served as the center of Athens, some activities becoming less common with time and others more common.

The remains are illuminated and often identified on the basis of the rich written documentation we have for Athens, unparalleled for any other Greek city: more than 700 literary references for the Agora alone, along with some 7,500 inscriptions found in the excavations. Supplemented by these written sources, the excavations have shed light on almost all facets of the ancient city – urban design, politics, military activity, athletics, commerce, religion, and memorials.

What follows here is a brief general summary of many of these elements; the rest of the volume is given over to individual essays emphasizing both past and current research on these and related topics.

City Planning and Urban Design

The city itself is totally dry and not well-watered, and badly laid out on account of its antiquity. Many of the houses are shabby, only a few useful. Seen by a stranger, it would at first be doubtful that this was the famed city of the Athenians.

(Pseudo-Dikaiarchos, *FGrH* 59)

Before the area of the excavations became the Agora, the space was used as a burial ground in the Bronze Age (3000–1100 B.C.) and for both burials and habitation in the Iron Age (1100–700 B.C.). Some 50 Bronze Age graves, mostly chamber tombs, have been excavated, but only six wells, which suggests very limited habitation north of the Acropolis. For the Iron Age, discovery of 85 graves and 45 wells seems to indicate both increased population and exploitation of the area for habitation.

As a city, Athens was known for a lack of urban planning and design, a circumstance attributed to the city's great antiquity. Generally, the excavations have confirmed this picture. When this part of Athens was given over to public rather than private use, the development seems to have been gradual and almost haphazard. Throughout the second and third quarters of the 6th century B.C. the wells, which suggest the locations of private houses in the area, were abandoned and filled in.

The earliest public development seems to be the establishment of an old line of communication as the major street of Athens, leading from the city gates at the northwest up to the Acropolis. Among other uses, this broad street carried the great Panathenaic procession in honor of Athena and therefore has become known as the Panathenaic Way. The organization of the festival on a grand scale is usually attributed to the tyrant Peisistratos in the year 566 B.C., and this may well be when the street evolved into a major thoroughfare.

The next step was to provide the new public space with sufficient water, which was for the first time piped in to a small fountain house just west of the Panathenaic Way in ca. 530–520 B.C. Other structures – including an altar dedicated to the 12 gods of ancient Greece, which served as the central milestone of the city – were built at about the same time by the sons of Peisistratos.

Later, more buildings (the Old Bouleuterion [council house] and perhaps the Royal Stoa) were added to serve the new democracy created in 508/7 B.C., and the public space was defined by a series of boundary stones. At about the same time, water management problems were solved by the construction of a monumental stone drain (the Great Drain), which carried surplus water down to the Eridanos River.

Aside from these relatively simple arrangements of traffic control, water supply, and water control, however, the Agora seems to have been allowed to develop piecemeal as buildings were added one by one to the periphery of the square throughout the Classical period (Fig. 1). In general the buildings housing the government were surprisingly modest in construction: walls of stone and/or mud brick, columns of limestone, floors of packed clay, and roofs of terracotta tiles were the norm (Tholos, Bouleuterion, Royal Stoa, South Stoa I, Square Peristyle). When the Athenian people built for themselves, they did not waste any money. Marble, sculptural adornment, and costly materials were largely reserved for the gods, both in the Agora (Stoa of Zeus, Hephaisteion) and elsewhere. And, despite its prominence, at all periods the Panathenaic Way was unpaved for

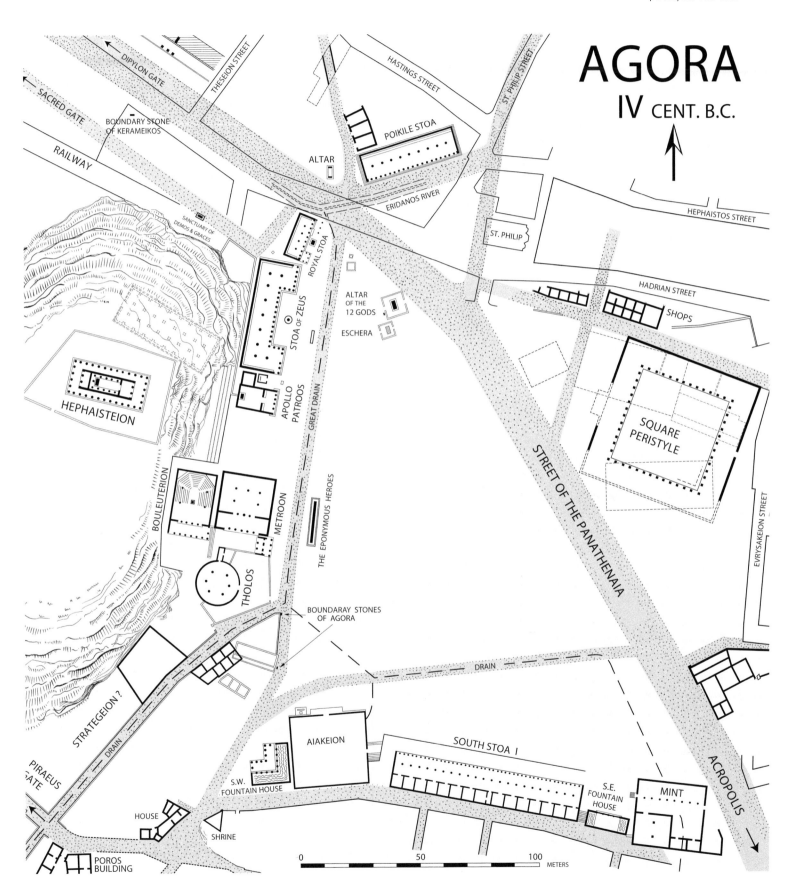

Fig. 1
The Agora in the Classical
period, ca. 400 B.C.

AGORA
IV CENT. B.C.

DIPYLON GATE

THESEION STREET

HASTINGS STREET

ST. PHILIP STREET

SACRED GATE

BOUNDARY STONE
OF KERAMEIKOS

RAILWAY

POIKILE STOA

ALTAR

ERIDANOS RIVER

ST. PHILIP

HEPHAISTOS STREET

SANCTUARY OF
DEMOS & GRACES

ROYAL STOA

STOA OF ZEUS

ALTAR
OF THE
12 GODS

ESCHERA

HADRIAN STREET

SHOPS

HEPHAISTEION

APOLLO PATROOS

GREAT DRAIN

SQUARE
PERISTYLE

BOULEUTERION

METROON

THE EPONYMOUS HEROES

STREET OF THE PANATHENAIA

EVRYSAKEION STREET

THOLOS

BOUNDARAY STONES
OF AGORA

DRAIN

STRATEGEION ?

DRAIN

ACROPOLIS

PIRAEUS GATE

AIAKEION

SOUTH STOA I

S.W.
FOUNTAIN HOUSE

S.E.
FOUNTAIN
HOUSE

MINT

HOUSE

SHRINE

0   50   100
                    METERS

POROS
BUILDING

Fig. 2
Model of the Agora in
ca. 400 B.C., view from
the southeast.

almost its entire length, surfaced only with successive layers of packed gravel (Fig. 2).

Aqueducts and fountains were added later to provide public water, though at all times the Athenians tapped subterranean sources by sinking wells into the underlying bedrock. Cisterns designed to store rainwater caught on roofs also became common in the Hellenistic period. In all, more than 400 wells and 150 cisterns, serving both public buildings and the surrounding private houses, have been excavated.

Only in the Hellenistic period, when regular squares lined with colonnades became popular in the Greek East (Ephesos, Priene, Miletos), is there some hint of planning in the Athenian Agora and some elegance to the buildings. The great stoas added in the mid-2nd century B.C. (Middle Stoa, Stoa of Attalos, and South Stoa II) were laid out in relation to one another, while a new archive building (the Metroon) along the old west side of the square was provided with an answering colonnaded

facade of marble (Fig. 3). By and large, however, the development and growth of the Classical Agora conforms to the untidy reputation of the city in antiquity.

The construction of the Middle Stoa effectively destroyed the integrity of the old square, which had been maintained for centuries. From the mid-2nd century B.C. on, however, the square was divided into two, and even the old boundary stones were completely obscured. The larger, northern part of the square was further compromised at the end of the 1st century B.C. Many of the functions of the old center were transferred to the new Market of Caesar and Augustus built some 100 meters to the east, and the last of the open space in the Classical Agora was filled with the construction of a huge *odeion* (concert hall) and a temple dedicated to Ares, the god of war (Fig. 4). And when Athens was rebuilt after the Herulian sack of A.D. 267, the old civic center was not even included within the fortified limits of the new city.

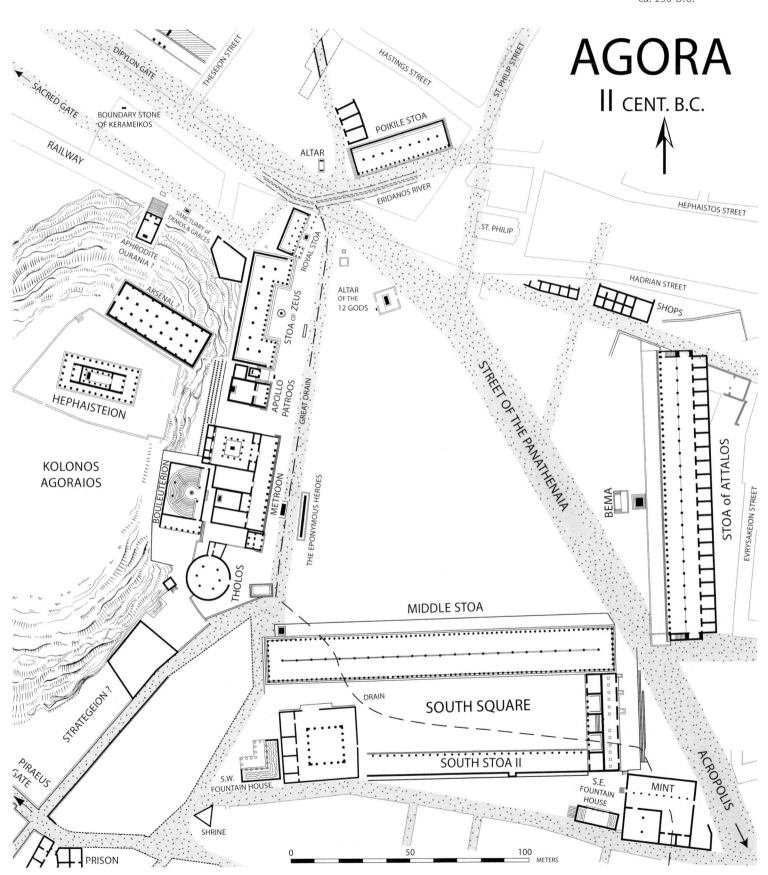

Fig. 3
The Agora in the
Hellenistic period,
ca. 150 B.C.

AGORA

II CENT. B.C.

THESEION STREET

DIPYLON GATE

HASTINGS STREET

ST. PHILIP STREET

SACRED GATE

BOUNDARY STONE
OF KERAMEIKOS

RAILWAY

POIKILE STOA

ALTAR

ERIDANOS RIVER

HEPHAISTOS STREET

ST. PHILIP

SANCTUARY of
DEMOS & GRACES

ROYAL STOA

APHRODITE
OURANIA ?

HADRIAN STREET

ARSENAL ?

STOA of ZEUS

ALTAR
OF THE
12 GODS

SHOPS

HEPHAISTEION

APOLLO
PATROOS

GREAT DRAIN

KOLONOS
AGORAIOS

BOULEUTERION

METROON

THE EPONYMOUS HEROES

STREET OF THE PANATHENAIA

BEMA

STOA of ATTALOS

EVRYSAKEION STREET

THOLOS

STRATEGEION ?

MIDDLE STOA

PIRAEUS
GATE

DRAIN

SOUTH SQUARE

ACROPOLIS

SOUTH STOA II

S.W.
FOUNTAIN HOUSE

S.E.
FOUNTAIN
HOUSE

MINT

SHRINE

0   50   100
METERS

PRISON

Fig. 4
The Agora at the height of its
development, ca. A.D. 150.

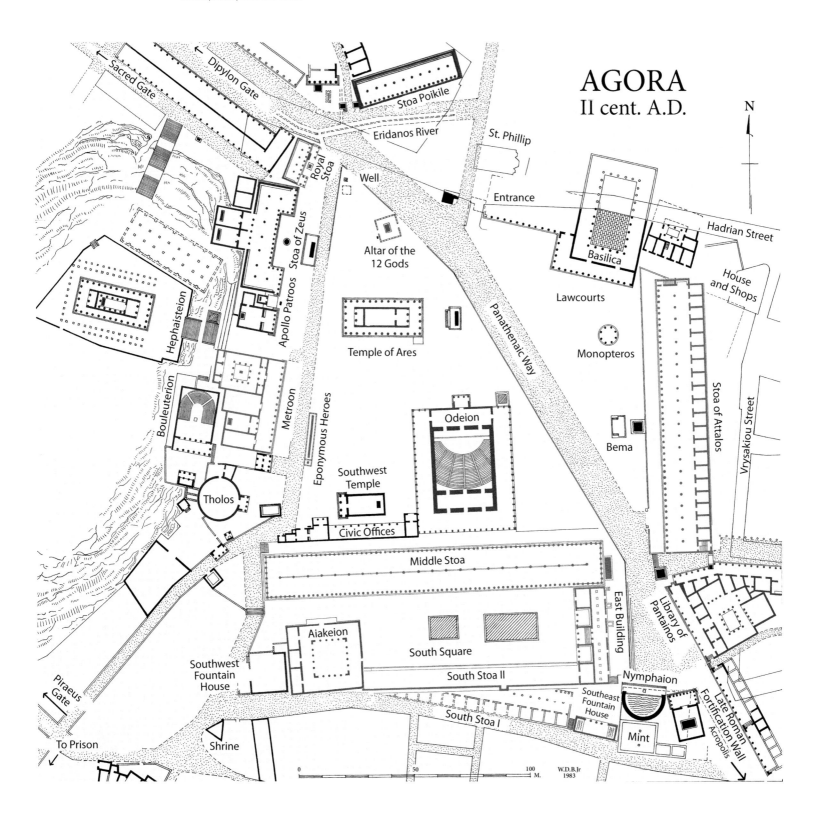

AGORA
II cent. A.D.

N

Sacred Gate

Dipylon Gate

Stoa Poikile

Eridanos River

St. Phillip

Royal Stoa

Well

Entrance

Hadrian Street

Apollo Patroos

Stoa of Zeus

Altar of the
12 Gods

Basilica

House
and Shops

Hephaisteion

Lawcourts

Temple of Ares

Monopteros

Bouleuterion

Metroon

Eponymous Heroes

Odeion

Bema

Stoa of Attalos

Vrysakiou Street

Southwest
Temple

Tholos

Civic Offices

Middle Stoa

East Building

Library of
Pantainos

Piraeus
Gate

Aiakeion

South Square

South Stoa II

Southwest
Fountain
House

South Stoa I

Nymphaion

Southeast
Fountain
House

Late Roman Fortification Wall
Acropolis

To Prison

Shrine

Mint

0   50   100
M.

W.D.B.Jr
1983

Civic Life and Politics

You will find everything sold together in the same place in Athens: figs, summoners, grapes, turnips, pears, apples, witnesses, roses, medlars, haggis, honeycombs, chickpeas, lawsuits, beestings [first milk], beestings-pudding, myrtle, allotment machines, hyacinth, lambs, waterclocks, laws, indictments.

(Athenaios 14.640b–c)

The Agora excavations have produced both buildings and objects that illustrate the workings of the most famous democracy of antiquity. Like the American version, Athenian democratic government was divided into three parts – executive, legislative, and judiciary – the major difference being that all three branches were staffed by Athenians in rotation, with few professionals involved. The magistracies, deliberative bodies, and courts were all made up of citizens, usually allotted to their positions for a year. A very few positions requiring expertise (generals, treasurers, and water commissioners) could not be left to the luck of the draw and

had to be filled by election. Slaves held the permanent or semipermanent positions occupied by professional bureaucrats today.

For the executive branch, the most significant building uncovered is surely the Stoa Basileios (Royal Stoa), headquarters of the archon basileus, a yearly-allotted magistrate, second in command of the Athenian government, who was responsible for laws and religious matters. He and his assistants were provided with a small stoa at the northwest corner of the Agora square, constructed following the Doric order of Greek architecture (Fig. 5). The date of the building is uncertain; it was clearly built or re-

Fig. 5
Model of the Royal Stoa,
ca. 500–400 B.C.

Fig. 6
Ruins of the Royal Stoa,
view from the south.

Fig. 7
The Tholos / Bouleuterion complex.

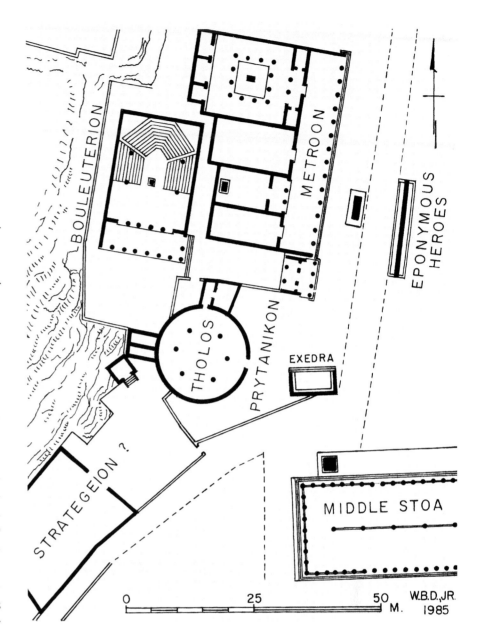

built after the Persian sack of Athens in 480/79 B.C. The identification is secure, however, based on the description of the traveler Pausanias (ca. A.D. 150) and two inscribed bases carrying dedications to king archons found on the steps of the building itself (Fig. 6). The identification of the building allows us to recognize the place which housed the oath-stone of the Athenians, the inscribed constitution of ca. 400 B.C., and the spot where Sokrates was indicted in 399 B.C. for impiety and other offenses.

The legislative branch is represented by two successive council chambers (Old [ca. 500 B.C.] and New [ca. 415 B.C.] Bouleuterion) and the senate dining chamber (Tholos) (Fig. 7). A senate (*boule*) of 500 citizens, 50 members from each of the 10 tribes, was empanelled for a year and met in the Bouleuterion every day except festivals to propose legislation to the people (*demos*). The full citizen body would meet in assembly (*ekklesia*) about every 10 days at the Pnyx to vote on the legislation proposed by the boule. Each tribal contingent of 50 served in rotation as the executive committee (*prytaneis*) of the boule and had the Tholos as its headquarters (Fig. 8). This was an unusual round building, dating to 470 B.C., which served primarily as the dining hall of the prytaneis, who were originally fed a modest meal in the building, probably cheese, barley cakes, olives, leeks, and wine (Fig. 9). In addition, one-third of the 50 members of the prytaneis were expected to sleep in the building every night, so if an emergency arose there were always 17 citizens on duty as senators at all times. In a sense, the Tholos thus represents the heart of the democracy. Its significance was not lost on the 30 Tyrants; installed by Sparta after victory in the Peloponne-

Fig. 8
Model of the Tholos, ca. 470 B.C.

Fig. 9
Pottery from the Tholos
inscribed with a delta/
epsilon ligature for
«demosion» (public prop-
erty), 5th century B.C.

Fig. 10
A law court at the
northeast corner of the
Agora square. Drawing by
R. Townsend.

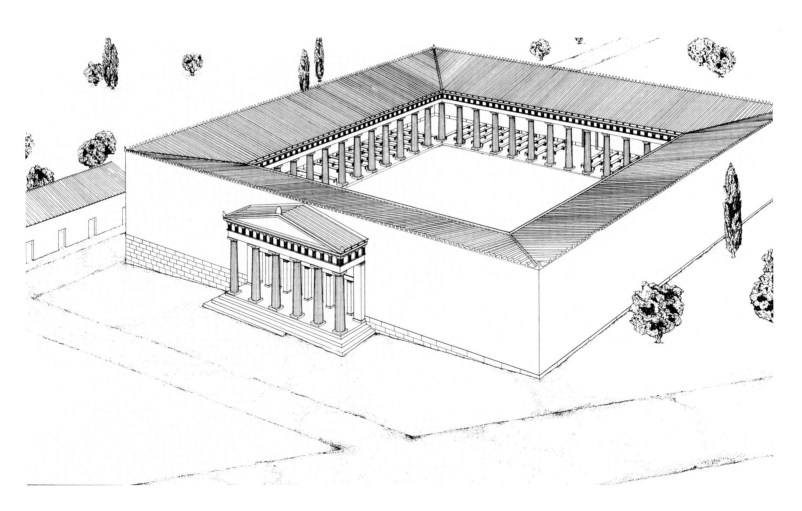

sian War in 404/3 B.C., they chose the Tholos as their headquarters.

The judiciary is represented by a series of 4th-century B.C. buildings which were later buried under the north end of the Stoa of Attalos. They are large enclosures open to the sky, sometimes ringed with interior colonnades, designed to house the usual Athenian juries of 201 or 501 men (Fig. 10). Their identification as law courts seems certain, as a crude terracotta box was found containing six bronze ballots used by the jurors (*dikasts*) to record their verdict (Fig. 11). The ballots take the form of round disks with a central axle — either pierced (guilty) or solid (innocent) — bearing the inscription «public vote» (Fig. 12). Other equipment has been found which sheds light on Athenian legal procedure. Most impressive, probably, are the *kleroteria* (allotment machines) used to choose a jury out of a pool of about 6,000 candidates available in any given year (Fig. 13). As in many countries today, the courts had the final say in how laws were to be interpreted and applied, and the Athenians went to great lengths to ensure that the juries were not subjected to undue influence. The machines, described by Aristotle, guaranteed equal tribal representation on every jury as well as completely random order in the way in which individual jurors were selected. The only way to bribe an Athenian jury was to pay all 6,000 potential jurors. A unique example of a waterclock reflects the daily workings of the

Fig. 11
Ballot box made of two drain tiles set on end, found at the northeast corner of the Agora, under the Stoa of Attalos, 4th century B.C.

Fig. 12
Bronze ballots found in the ballot box, 4th century B.C., inscribed «psephos demosion» (public ballot); note solid axle (at left) and hollow axle (at right).

Fig. 13
A «kleroterion» (allotment machine) used to pick Athenian jurors in a random selection. The slots are to hold jurors' bronze allotment plates; the cuttings at the left held a hollow bronze tube that dispensed black and white marbles to determine which horizontal row was picked or rejected for jury duty.

court (Fig. 14). A simple deep bowl, near the rim it has an overflow hole and at the bottom an outlet hole through which the water escaped; the speaker simply continued until time literally ran out.

Ostracism, a convenient way to vote a politician out of office, was also a feature of public life in the Agora. Once a year the citizens would gather in the square to vote on a simple yes-or-no question: «Does anybody represent a threat to the democracy?» If a simple majority voted «yes», the Athenians met again in the Agora several weeks later, each bringing a broken piece of pottery (*ostrakon*) on which he had inscribed a name (Fig. 15). The man named on the most ostraka lost, and he was exiled for 10 years. This was an efficient and immediate means of removing a troublesome individual from the political arena, and many prominent statesmen in the 5th century B.C. took one of these «extended vacations» courtesy of the Athenian people. Once cast and counted, these informal ceramic ballots were used to fill potholes or to grade streets, or were discarded wherever possible. More than 1,500 have been found in the Agora, providing a vivid picture both of the uncertainty of public life in Athens and of the care the Athenians took to safeguard their democracy. Some further ways in which this class of artifact sheds light on the intricacies of Athenian democracy are discussed by James Sickinger in Chapter 7.

Fig. 14
A «klepsydra» (water-clock) used to time speeches in the Athenian courts.

Fig. 15
«Ostraka» (inscribed potsherds) used as ballots to exile prominent politicians. The two shown here read «Kallixenos the Traitor» (left) and «Out with Themistokles» (right).

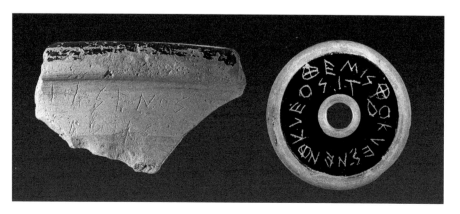

Commerce

Each of you is in the habit of frequenting some place, a perfumer's shop, a barber's, a cobbler's, and so forth; and the greatest number visit those who have their establishments nearest the agora, the smallest number those who are farthest from it.

(Lysias 24.20)

The Athenian Agora was also a great center of commercial activity, housed in a wide array of buildings. Great advances have been made in our understanding of these functions in recent years, as discussed by Susan Rotroff in Chapter 2. It is now clear that all manner of trade and commerce occurred in and around the square. Dozens of commodities are listed in the literary sources as having been sold in the Agora: flour, bread, fish, meat, birds, cheese, vegetables, garlic, onions, olives, wine, wreaths, and leather, to name just a few. Many of these arrived at the Agora in ceramic transport vessels, amphoras, whose importance for understanding the history of the Agora is discussed by Mark Lawall in Chapter 5. The archaeological evidence from nearby workshops preserves evidence of other manufacturers and shopkeepers: sculptors, potters, makers of terracotta figurines, bronze-casters, shoemakers, wine merchants, and bone-workers.

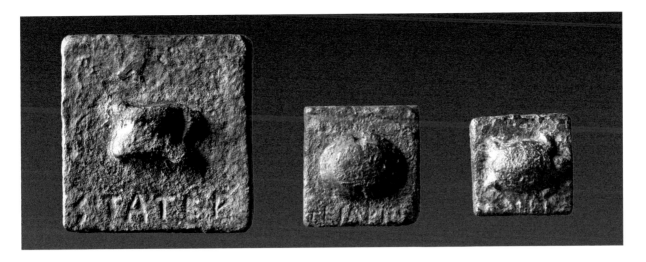

State officials charged with regulating the market included those responsible for weights and
measures (*metronomoi*), who used official sets of
bronze weights and both terracotta and bronze measures to ensure that commodities were fairly traded
(Fig. 16). These were either inscribed or stamped
to indicate that they were official, and the bronze
weights are paralleled by lead examples actually used
on a day-to-day basis by individual merchants. The
dry measures were used for grain and nuts, while a
series of liquid measures were presumably used for
wine and olive oil (Fig. 17). An inscription suggests
that the metronomoi sat in South Stoa I, a long
colonnade that closed the south side of the square
and seems to have served as the headquarters for
several other commercial boards as well (Fig. 18).
A second set of official weights is known to have
been kept in the Tholos, near which was also found

a marble slab carved to show the shape and size of
standard terracotta roof tiles.

A reliable supply and distribution of grain in order
to feed the huge population of Athens was a constant
concern, and boards of officials known as *sitophy-
lakes, agoranomoi,* and *epimeletes* of the *emborio*
(market) were all concerned with its regulation.
A stoa where barley was sold that is referred to by
Aristophanes (*Ekklesiazousai* 11.684–686) seems
to have stood in or near the Agora and may be associated with South Stoa I. In the 4th century B.C.,
grain brought up from Piraeus was stored and sold
at the old sanctuary of Aiakos (also known as the
Aiakeion), now identified as the large enclosure at
the southwest corner of the Agora (Fig. 19). And
small enclosures (*telia*) made of wooden boards were
used to hold grain or flour sold in the Agora (Schol.
Aristophanes, *Plutus* 1037, *Etym. Magnum*).

The excavations have also brought to light more than 70,000 coins – mostly bronze – which circulated in the marketplace. Athenian silver coinage was minted with metal extracted from the rich mines at Laurion in southern Attica and was widely circulated throughout the Mediterranean. Despite changes of size and style, the coins always featured the head of Athena on one side and her sacred bird, the owl, on the reverse (Fig. 20). The circulation of counterfeit money was a concern, and a law passed in 375/4 B.C. establishes official testers at the bankers' tables to ensure the purity of the coins in circulation. A handful of fake silver coins, withdrawn from circulation and slashed to expose their impurity, have been found, along with some made of lead. One of the mints for Athenian coinage has been recognized at the southeast corner of the square. It was used only for the production of bronze coinage in the 3rd and 2nd centuries B.C. The identification is based largely on dozens of unstruck bronze coin blanks and fragments of the rods from which they were cut (Fig. 21). Athenian silver coinage predates the building (ca. 400 B.C.) by several decades, so we have to imagine that the silver coinage was minted elsewhere. The discovery of a large number of bronze coins in the adjacent South Stoa I suggests that the new bronze coinage was put into circulation there and that the south side of the square served as the commercial center of the Agora.

Less official commercial buildings surrounded the Agora: a row of small square rooms, each with a

Fig. 19
Plan of the south side of the Agora, showing the Aiakeion, South Stoa I, and Mint. The Athenian Agora was also a great center of commercial activity, housed in a wide array of buildings.

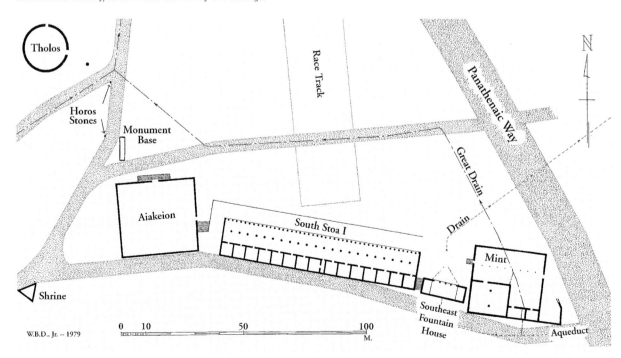

door opening directly off a street or perhaps grouped along either side of a common interior passageway. Their prominent locations and fairly substantial construction make it uncertain whether they were entirely public or private enterprises, though it seems clear that they were commercial in function. More informal still are individual rooms attached to private houses but with a separate door opening directly onto a street, often with no direct access into the house. Even less substantial were the temporary wicker booths and tents set up in the Agora for market activities, leaving little or nothing in the archaeological record but attested in several ancient sources.

A far more substantial building for commerce was erected in the Agora in the Hellenistic period. The Stoa of Attalos, built for the Athenians by Attalos II of Pergamon (159–138 B.C.) closed off the east side of the square (Fig. 22). Well over 100 meters long, it was two-storeyed, with a double colonnade in front of 21 shops on each floor — very much the predecessor of its modern counterpart, the shopping mall (Fig. 23). It served as the main commercial building in the Agora for some 400 years, until it was destroyed in the Herulian sack of A.D. 267. More commercial activity may also have been accommodated in two other stoas, known as the Middle Stoa and South Stoa II, constructed in the southern part of the square at about the same time; more modestly built and lacking rooms, they would have sheltered more ephemeral market installations and activity.

In the late 1st century B.C., the Agora lost some of its commercial importance, as much business was transferred to the new Market of Caesar and Augustus, built about 100 meters to the east. By the 2nd century A.D., the old Greek Agora was known as the *Kerameikos*, taking its name from the neighboring potters' quarter of which it had been a part for centuries.

⇧ Fig. 20
Three silver Athenian coins with the head of Athena on the obverse, and her sacred owl on the reverse.

Fig. 21
Bronze rod and coin blanks from the building in the southeastern corner of the Agora identified as the Mint. These represent one of the early stages in the production of bronze coinage in the Hellenistic period.

Fig. 22
Reconstruction of the Stoa of Attalos. The original dates to ca. 150 B.C.

Fig. 23
Interior view of the reconstructed Stoa of Attalos. The building originally contained 42 shops on two levels under a single roof.

Military Activity

Go forth from the chambers roofed with cypress wood, Manes; go to the agora, to the Herms, the place frequented by the phylarchs, and to their handsome pupils, whom Pheidon trains in mounting and dismounting.

(Athenaios 9.402f)

Although the backbone of Athenian military prowess was the city's great fleet, housed in the three harbors of Piraeus, the land army was administered in large part from the Agora. Lists of military conscriptions of new recruits (*ephebes*) and Mobilization orders for citizens were posted at the Monument of the Eponymous Heroes, which served as a public notice board (Fig. 24). According to Aeschines (*De falsa legatione* 2.85), the headquarters of the 10 elected generals, the Strategeion, stood in or near the Agora. A possible candidate for this structure has been located just southwest of the Tholos; very poorly preserved, it takes the form of several rooms grouped around a central courtyard. Susan Rotroff discusses the identification of this building and recent discoveries in Chapter 2.

More certain is a large body of material concerning the management of the Athenian cavalry which has been recovered at the northwest corner of the Agora. Reliefs showing cavalry contingents, honorary decrees for the *hipparchs* and *phylarchs* (cavalry commanders), tokens, and part of an archive all cluster together, suggesting that somewhere nearby should be the Hipparcheion (headquarters of the cavalry commanders), though no specific remains have been identified. The archive consists of several dozen lead strips each incised with a man's name and a description of the horse (color, brand, value) he presented to officials to demonstrate his right to fight with the cavalry, which in Athens, as elsewhere throughout history, has always been an elite force. The value listed indicated the amount the owner would be reimbursed if he lost his horse in battle (Fig. 25). Also recovered were several lead tokens, each carrying a representation of a piece of armor: shield, helmet, breastplate, or greaves. These could apparently be redeemed for actual armor when the army was mobilized (Fig. 26). Finally, more than a dozen stamped clay disks were recovered, carrying the name of Pheidon, the hipparch in Lemnos (an Athenian island possession administered by the army) (Fig. 27). Stamped before they were fired, these tokens were probably used to establish the credentials of a messenger or anyone else in possession of a token as an official representative of the hipparch Pheidon. The fragment of the 4th-century B.C. comic poet Mnesimachos, preserved in Athenaios and quoted earlier, thus preserves an

Fig. 24

Model of the Monument of the Eponymous Heroes, ca. 330 B.C. Lists of military conscriptions of new recruits («ephebes») and mobilization orders for citizens were posted below the statues, which represented the 10 tribes to which Kleisthenes assigned all Athenians when he created the democracy in 508/7 B.C.

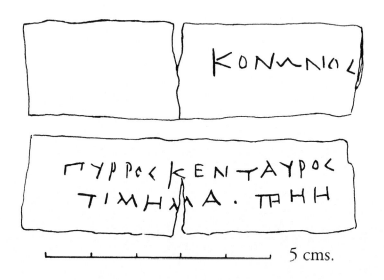

KONΛΛΝOL

ΓYPPOℂ ΚΕΝΤΑΥΡOℂ
ΤΙΜΗΛΛΑ . ⅢΗΗ

5 cms.

Fig. 25
An inscribed lead tablet from the cavalry archive,
4th–3rd century B.C. (drawing, photograph). The text reads,
«of Konon, a chestnut with a centaur [brand], value
700 drachmas».

⇩ Fig. 26
Lead tokens for the
distribution of pieces of
armor, 3rd century B.C.

extraordinary correlation between literature and archaeology. The herms were a series of primitive statues set up at the northwest entrance to the Agora, just where the clay tokens issued by Pheidon were found in a well. The large open space of the Agora and the wide surface of the Panathenaic Way at this point were apparently a convenient and useful place to train and exercise the cavalry. The people of Elis, according to Pausanias (6.24.2), even called their agora «the Hippodrome» because they also used it for training horses. Similar clay tokens for another military official, the commander of the border patrol (*peripolarch*) Xenokles, have also been found in the excavations (Fig. 28).

Fig. 27
Clay tokens stamped with the name and title of the cavalry commander («hipparch») in charge of the island of Lemnos, Pheidon of Thria, 4th century B.C.

Fig. 28
Clay tokens stamped with the name of the commander of the border patrol («peripolarch»), Xenokles of Perithoidai, 4th century B.C.

Athletics

You will find that at other cities statues of athletes are set up in the agoras, at Athens statues of good generals and tyrannicides.

(Lykourgos, *Leokrates* 51)

Despite this sentiment, athletic competition played an important role in Athenian life, as it did in any Greek city. In Athens, a festival in honor of Athena with a strong athletic component, the Panathenaia, was founded or reorganized on a grand scale by the tyrant Peisistratos in 566 B.C., some 200 years after the Olympics but only a decade or so after the origins of the other three Panhellenic games at Delphi, Isthmia, and Nemea. The program at Athens was different from the four Panhellenic games in several important respects: some contests were open only to Athenians, there were prizes of value, there were prizes for more than just first place, and there were team competitions. These last three aspects perhaps reflect the democratic politics of Athens, in contrast to the essentially aristocratic ethos of the Panhellenic games, with their emphasis on the individual. Though there were various prizes, including money and cattle for sacrifice and feasting, the most striking prize was olive oil taken

Fig. 29
Panathenaic amphora (P 24661) of the late 6th century B.C.
for victory in the four-horse chariot race.

from Athena's sacred trees and delivered in specially made amphoras. Painted in the black-figured style, a Panathenaic amphora had a picture of Athena on one side and a depiction of the contest for which it was a prize on the other (Fig. 29).

It seems likely that there was a close relationship between the games and the Agora early on. One of the earliest public inscriptions from Athens, though fragmentary, seems to refer to a *dromos,* which means a racetrack, and it now seems likely that part of the unpaved Panathenaic Way, used as the processional route for the festival, also served as the racecourse for the games. Excavations have shown that the surfaces of the road in the 5th century B.C. were made of carefully screened material, with no stones at all, packed very smooth and very level, making an ideal running track. Later in the 5th century a simple starting line was added and the track deviated from the road and ran in a more southerly direction, across the open space of the Agora. The starting line, a set of square stone blocks with sockets for wooden posts, can be paralleled at Priene and Didyma, both in Asia Minor (Fig. 30). The change in orientation and/or location of a running track can be seen also at Olympia, Isthmia, Nemea, and Corinth. What is of particular interest is that the

Fig. 30
Stone sockets for wooden posts for the starting line of a race track through the Agora, late 5th century B.C.

only two other Classical agoras excavated in Greece, at Corinth and Argos, both have racetracks as well and it can be argued that the initial laying out of a large open space in the middle of a Greek city was originally intended to serve as an athletic venue, and that most of the other uses for an agora come later.

In the 330s B.C. a proper stadium was constructed southeast of the Acropolis and most events of the Panathenaic games were transferred there, with the equestrian events held at the hippodrome near the sea at Phaleron. The *anthippasia,* a team event involving contingents of cavalry divided by tribes, was probably held in the hippodrome, although the victory monuments were set up by the winning tribe in the Agora (Fig. 31). One very old-fashioned event, the *apobates,* continued to be held in the Agora square, however. This race involved a man in armor jumping on and off a moving chariot driven by a second man (Fig. 32). The finish line seems to have been the Eleusinion, just southeast of the square. The origin of this unusual event must be very early since there is little evidence that the Classical Athenians used chariots in warfare during the historical period, nor does this event appear on the program of any of the Panhellenic games.

Fig. 31
Fragment of a sculpted monument commemorating a tribal victory in the «anthippasia» (team cavalry display) at the Panathenaic games, ca. 400 B.C. (I 7167).

Fig. 32
Base for a monument commemorating a victory in the «apobates», showing the chariot and armed warrior, 4th century B.C. (S 399).

Religion and Cult

*Men of Athens, I perceive that in every way you are very religious. For as I passed along,
and observed the objects of your worship, I found also an altar with this inscription,
«To an unknown god».*

(Acts of the Apostles 17)

Though the Acropolis was the major focal point for the great temples dedicated to Athena, the Agora was also a center of cult activity, crowded with appropriate buildings. These range in magnificence from the marble Doric masterpiece, the Hephaisteion (Temple of Hephaistos), crowning the hill to the west, to the smallest and simplest of altars. There was no separation of church and state in those days, and almost all activities, public and private, were conducted under the auspices and protection of the gods. Much of the law code displayed at the Royal Stoa was in fact a sacred calendar, listing the dates and specifications of sacrifices the state was required to carry out in honor of various deities. The Panathenaia and other large festivals had numerous components, including sacrifices, feasting, lavish processions, dramatic performances, athletic contests, and torch races. Many of these events took place in, or passed through, the great open square of the Agora, which took on a holiday atmosphere as the whole population shared in the religious life of the city. More than 20 gods and 8 heroes are known to have been honored in the Agora, in temples and open-air sanctuaries, through inscribed altars and dedications.

The physical center of Athens and its zero milestone was the Altar of the Twelve Gods, established in the Agora by the younger Peisistratos in 522/1 B.C. (Fig. 33). As mentioned earlier, the northwest entrance into the square was also marked with dozens of herms, primitive portraits of Hermes, the god of doorways, trade, commerce, and thieves, and thus a worthy patron of the marketplace; an altar of Hermes Agoraios stood nearby (Fig. 34). Another monument, which reflected an individual's legal identity and provided every Athenian citizen with a heroic ancestor, was the Monument of the Eponymous Heroes (also mentioned earlier), carrying statues of the 10 heroes after whom the 10 tribes of Athens were named at the time of the foundation of the democracy.

During the Roman period, the worship of emperors became a necessity and several new temples were erected in and around the square. Rather than build entirely new temples, the Athenians went out to the outlying and largely deserted villages and sanctuaries of Attica (Thorikos, Sounion, Pallene, and perhaps Brauron), disassembled the old neglected Classical temples still standing there, transported

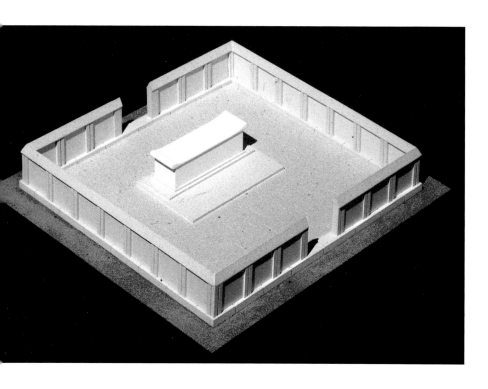

Fig. 33
Model of the Altar of the Twelve Gods, established in the Agora by the younger Peisistratos in 522/1 B.C.

them piece by piece, and reerected them in downtown Athens.

Christianity did not have an easy time in Athens. Paul spoke there with only limited success before moving on to Corinth. And despite official disapproval, pagan cults flourished even after the emperor Constantine converted to Christianity in the 4th century A.D. The philosophical schools, several lying just south of the Agora, provided much of the resistance, tracing their ancestry to the old gymnasia and worshipping Hermes, Herakles, the Muses, and the Nymphs. It took an imperial decree to stop them in A.D. 529, when Justinian forbade any pagan to teach philosophy in Athens.

Fig. 34
Heads of herms found at the northwest corner of the Agora.

Education and Philosophy

Early in the morning he [Sokrates] used to go to the walkways and gymnasia, to appear in the agora as it filled up, and to be present wherever he would meet with the most people.

(Xenophon, *Memorabilia* 1.1.10).

Though the first established schools of philosophy, the Academy and the Lyceum, were founded in old gymnasia outside the city's walls, at all times the Agora served also as a center of learning. Sokrates much preferred to teach among crowds: «If you hear me making my defense in the same language I customarily use both elsewhere and in the agora at the tables where many of you have heard me, do not marvel or raise a clamor on this account» (Plato, *Apology* 17c). In addition to the bankers' tables, which may well have been set up at or near South Stoa I, another of Sokrates' informal classrooms has been recognized just between the Tholos and an Agora boundary stone. This is a modest house of the 5th century B.C. which, to judge from iron hobnails, bone eyelets, and part of an inscribed cup found there, housed a shoemaker named Simon. According to Xenophon (*Memorabilia* 4.2), Sokrates used Simon's shop when he wished to meet students who were too young to go into the Agora. Other Agora buildings associated with Sokrates include the Royal Stoa, headquarters of the king archon, where Sokrates was indicted in 399 B.C., and – less probably identified – the prison where he was held before his execution by poison. More about Simon's house and the residential aspects of the Agora can be found in Chapter 3 by Barbara Tsakirgis.

Sokrates is not the only philosopher associated with the site. Diogenes the Cynic, living in conspicuous poverty in and around the Agora, is said to have slept in a *pithos* (a large storage jar) in the Metroon. When Zeno came to Athens from Cyprus late in the 4th century B.C., he also preferred the Agora over the gymnasia and chose as his meeting place the old Painted Stoa along the north side of the square. From this classroom in the stoa, he and his followers became known as the Stoics.

Athens never lost its dominant position in education; philosophers and their students flocked to the city from all over the Mediterranean throughout the Hellenistic period. The benefits to the city are clear. The Ptolemies of Egypt built a fine new gymnasium, for example, and the Stoa of Attalos was given by a grateful king of Pergamon, who had studied in Athens under the philosopher Karneades. The same tradition was carried on throughout the Roman period, and the archaeology accurately mirrors this educational significance. One of the buildings added to the Agora in about A.D. 100 was a library built by a local Athenian, Titus Flavius Pantainos, who describes himself as a priest of the «philosophical Muses» and the son of Flavius Menander, the head of a philosophical school. In the middle of the 2nd century A.D. the large odeion built by Agrippa was converted into a lecture hall for philosophical discourse (Philostratos, *Vit. Soph.* 571, 597). Later still, in the 4th and 5th centuries A.D., the slopes of the hill south of the Agora were crowded with large and elegant villas, several of them clearly used as private philosophical schools which flourished until they were shut down by Justinian in A.D. 529.

Dramatic Performances and Spectacles

The ikria [grandstands] were constructed as far as this [poplar] tree; they were upright timbers,
with planks attached to them, like steps; on these planks the audience sat, before the theater was built.

(Hesychius)

The large open square, capable of holding thousands of people, was a natural venue for large-scale spectacles of various types. These were often performed as part of a religious festival. Early on, for instance, the Agora was used as a venue for dramatic performances, and a part of the square was known as the *orchestra* (dancing ground). The seating for spectators consisted of large temporary wooden structures of scaffolding, known in Greek as *ikria* and in colloquial English as «bleachers». When a set of these collapsed during a dramatic performance in the early 5th century B.C., we are told, the plays were transferred to the sanctuary of Dionysos, south of the Acropolis, where the theater is built into the slope of the hill.

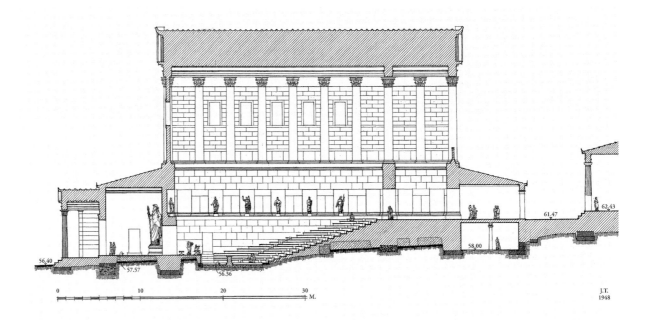

Fig. 35
Elevation of the Odeion,
late 1st century B.C.

Less formal entertainment is attested for the Classical period, when, we learn, jugglers and sword-swallowers, certain of an audience with time on its hands, would perform at the Painted Stoa.

In Roman times, performances in the Agora were accommodated in a lavish marble odeion built for the Athenians by Agrippa, son-in-law of the emperor Augustus, in the years around 15 B.C. A covered theater seating about a thousand people, it would have been used primarily for concerts and singing performances. It was set down in the middle of the old square, which it dominated by its large scale and great height (Fig. 35).

Perhaps the most compelling spectacle of all was the huge procession held as part of the Panathenaic festival in honor of Athena. The parade involved hundreds of individuals and animals, described by Aristophanes and depicted on the frieze which decorated the Parthenon: *kanephoroi* (aristocratic maidens carrying sacrificial paraphernalia), stool-bearers, water-bearers, parasol-bearers, musicians with flutes and *kitharas,* olive-branch-bearing elders, sacrificial cows and sheep, and a huge contingent of cavalry. All the participants would be elegantly dressed in their best finery and the display must have been magnificent as it made its way through the Agora and up the slopes to the Acropolis. The literary evidence suggests that this parade was held annually for about a thousand years, from the 6th century B.C. until at least the 4th century A.D. The Panathenaic Way, the broad route followed by the procession through the Agora, has been excavated at various points and some 66 superimposed layers have been recorded, also covering a period of about 1,000 years. Here, too, special temporary stands or *ikria* were set up along the course of the street to provide spectators with a good view as the parade went by. Cuttings for the supports have been excavated at the shoulder of the road at several points along its course through the Agora.

Memorial Display: Military

Pass on in thought to the Stoa Poikile too — the memorials of all your great deeds are set up in the Agora.

(Aeschines, *Ktesiphon* 3.186)

Not surprisingly, the Agora was also deemed the appropriate repository of innumerable monuments commemorating Athenian triumphs. Several buildings, as well as the square itself, were used for such display.

The Stoa Poikile (the Painted Stoa), built ca. 470 B.C., was used for the display of various military memorials (Fig. 36). The paintings described by the traveler Pausanias (ca. A.D. 150) showed Athenian military triumphs, both mythical and historical: the Athenians fighting Amazons, the fall of Troy, the victory over the Persians at Marathon, and the Athenians defeating the Spartans at Argive Oinoe. In a sense, the Painted Stoa may be thought of as an early museum, containing art on permanent public display. The paintings were exhibited in the Stoa for more than 600 years. The building also displayed more tangible evidence of Athenian triumphs: shields taken from the enemy in battle. Pausanias saw a group taken from the Spartans at Pylos (425/4 B.C.) and others from a victory at Skione (421 B.C.). One of the shields from Pylos, carrying the inscription «The Athenians from the Lacedaimonians at Pylos», has actually been recovered in the excavations (Fig. 37). Also from the Peloponnesian War is an inscribed bronze spear butt taken from the rebellious allies of Lesbos in 428 B.C. and dedicated to the Dioskouroi (the sons of Zeus, Castor and Pollux) (Fig. 38).

Other shields, those belonging to Athenians who died fighting for Athens, were displayed on a different building, the Stoa of Zeus Eleutherios (*eleutherios* means «freedom»). The wall of this stoa was also decorated with a painting of the Battle of Man-

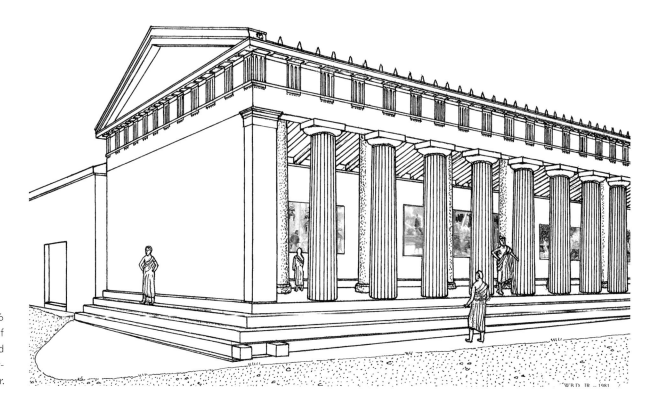

Fig. 36
Reconstruction drawing of
the Stoa Poikile (Painted
Stoa), ca. 470 B.C. Draw-
ing by W. B. Dinsmoor Jr.

tineia (362 B.C.), when the Athenians and their allies checked the rising power of Thebes.

Among the earliest known statues in the Agora are three of Hermes, known as herms, set up to commemorate victories in the aftermath of the Persian Wars. In the 5th century such memorials did not honor individuals; the name of Kimon did not appear on the three herms dedicated after the Battle of the Eurymedon (466 B.C.), and the name of his father Miltiades did not appear in the painting of the Battle of Marathon (490 B.C.) in the Painted Stoa. Things changed in the 4th century B.C., however, when statues of successful generals — Chabrias, Timotheos, Konon — were set up in the Agora square. In addition to military victories, which decreased significantly after the 4th century B.C., monuments celebrating victories in the military events of the Panathenaic games were also featured in the Agora. Especially common are memorials of the equestrian contests.

Fig. 37
Inscribed bronze shield
taken from the Spartans
in 425/4 B.C. after the
battle of Pylos in southwest
Greece (photograph, draw-
ing). The punched inscription reads, «The Athenians
from the Lacedaimonians
at Pylos».

Fig. 38
Bronze spear butt taken
from the inhabitants of
the island of Lesbos in
428 B.C. and dedicated
to the Dioskouroi (the
sons of Zeus, Castor and
Pollux) (B 1373).

Memorial Display: Public Honors

*Their benefactors they rewarded with the highest and most distinguished honors, setting them up in
bronze in the agora, and giving them a seat beside the gods on the Acropolis.*

(Aristeides 53.23–24)

The concept of personal honor was an extraordinarily important aspect of Classical Greece.
Just as athletes in the Panhellenic games competed
for nothing more than a wreath, so the Athenians
contended for recognition in the political arena. In
a society which had few tangible luxuries, honors
conferred by the state were coveted prizes. These
included wreaths and a public announcement of the
honor, a front-row seat at performances in the theater, and free meals at the Prytaneion (town hall). Of
more lasting significance was a record of the awards
granted, inscribed on a marble stele and displayed
in a conspicuous place. Especially noteworthy service could be rewarded with a statue in the Agora.
Because bronze can be melted down and reused,
only tiny fragments of such statues survive in the
Agora. Dozens of inscribed bases with cuttings for
such statues and numerous literary references allow
us to fill out the picture of this aspect of the appearance and use of the square.

The earliest such monument attested is a pair of
statues of the tyrant slayers Harmodios and Ari-
stogeiton erected in the Agora not far from where
they struck down the tyrant Hipparchos in 514 B.C.
Set up soon after the expulsion in 510 B.C. of the
surviving brother, Hippias, the original statues,
made by Antenor, were carried off by the Persians
in 480/79 B.C. and were soon replaced by a second
pair, made by Kritios, in 477 B.C. When Alexander conquered the Persians, he found the original
pair at Susa and sent it back to the Athenians, so
the two groups stood side by side thereafter. The
statues of both groups were of bronze and do not
survive, though several copies and representations
are known, along with a fragment of the marble base
for one of the groups, carrying a dedicatory epigram
which mentions Harmodios.

As time went on, Athens fell under the control
of the successors of Alexander the Great in what is
known as the Hellenistic period (the 3rd and 2nd
centuries B.C.). More and more, high Athenian
public honors such as statues became a tool in foreign policy. Hellenistic dynasts and kings controlling the vital grain supply in the northern Black Sea
became common recipients, reflecting the realities
of the times. Dozens of such statues were seen and
described by Pausanias as he made his way through
the area in the years around A.D. 150. His description of the statues and buildings he saw in the Agora
are one basis for many of our identifications today.
Detailed stylistic analysis is also used by researchers
to identify honorands and to reveal the possible reasons why a statue was dedicated. An example of this
approach is provided by Lee Ann Riccardi's study of
recently excavated Roman statuary in Chapter 4.

Lesser honors were available as well, particularly
to citizens who held a variety of positions: military
officers, officials in charge of the gymnasia, and

various magistrates. Seeing one's name publicly inscribed on a marble stele must have been a thrill, to judge from the hundreds recovered which list and praise ordinary citizens who served the government, however modestly. «For where the prizes offered for virtue are greatest, there are found the best citizens» (Thucydides 2.46). Through such honors, prominently displayed in the Agora, every Athenian was both reminded of a glorious past and encouraged to compete for similar recognition and honor.

Epilogue

From the 6th century B.C. until the 6th century A.D., the area of the Agora served as a focal point for the city of Athens, as the administrative/political center, as a venue for public performances, as a repository for collective memory, as a commercial hub, and as an educational beacon. The history of the city, its aspirations, and its achievements are written in the stratigraphy of the excavations.

The final phase of these large excavations is under way. As described in more detail by Craig Mauzy in Chapter 8, the original concession where work started in 1931 was limited on the north by the Athens – Piraeus railroad. When that proved insufficient for the recovery of the buildings lining the north side of the square, the excavations were carried farther north in 1969. Here the Royal Stoa, headquarters of the magistrate responsible for Athenian laws and site of the indictment of Sokrates for impiety, came to light, but not the northern limits of the square. A further northward advance was made in 1979, across modern Hadrian Street and the ancient Eridanos River. Here, at last, was found the western end of a large stoa closing the north side of the square, dating to the early 5th century B.C. and plausibly identified as the Painted Stoa.

Work in recent years has concentrated behind the Painted Stoa, revealing levels which date from the Bronze Age to the Byzantine period. The earliest signs of human activity take the form of two Mycenaean chamber tombs, dating to around 1350 B.C., each with multiple burials and an array of grave goods consisting of pottery, figurines, bronze weapons, and jewelry. They are followed by much poorer graves of the Iron Age (ca. 1100 B.C.), largely devoid of grave goods. There are few further signs of the use of the area until around 500 B.C., when a handsome marble altar, perhaps dedicated to Aphrodite Ourania (the «heavenly» one), was built. A large group of ostraka deposited in the area bears witness to the struggle for power in Athens in 484/3 B.C. between Themistokles and Xanthippos, father of Perikles, a contest which Xanthippos lost. A well, full of debris from a private house, reflects the destruction of Athens by the Persians in 480/79 B.C. Following this destruction, the Painted Stoa was built around 470 B.C. Behind it a modest shop was constructed in the late 5th century and remained in use at least until the 1st century A.D., with one or more of the shops selling terracotta figurines. A bath of the Roman period was the next major addition to the area, apparently destroyed by Alaric and the Visigoths in A.D. 395; recovery in the area was hindered by a further invasion by the Vandals, probably in the 460s A.D. Soon after, the area was abandoned but, in the years around A.D. 1000, the city expanded and thus this area once again became a crowded neighborhood.

With the completion of excavation of this area and of the remainder of the Painted Stoa, following the removal of two more modern buildings and a stretch of Hadrian Street, the American School will have fulfilled its original commitment to the people of Greece: the excavation of the Agora square and the public buildings around it. This task, along with conservation, research, and publication, may well carry the project to its 100th anniversary.

Commerce and Crafts around the Athenian Agora

by Susan I. Rotroff

Much attention has been lavished on the political character of the Agora of Athens, and certainly the primary motive for undertaking the daunting task of excavation in the middle of the modern city was the identification of the site that hosted Europe's first democracy. Ancient authors mention the Agora and its surrounding public buildings time and time again as the venue of important historical events and political activities. But the space had another function as well, and one that was equally important for the well-being of the city: it was a center of commerce. This role survives in the modern Greek language; if you hop into an Athenian taxi and give «agora» as your destination, you will find yourself in the central produce markets of the city, some 600 meters to the northeast of the ancient city center that you perhaps had intended to visit.

By the Hellenistic period this commercial aspect had been formalized, and around the middle of the 2nd century B.C. King Attalos, ruler of the wealthy kingdom of Pergamon in Asia Minor, presented Athens with a large and lavish shop building, known as the Stoa of Attalos. Marble-faced and some 116 meters in length, it housed 42 shops on two floors, fronted by wide colonnades for shelter from rain and sun. It was a very useful gift: the people of Athens could enjoy convenient covered shopping, and the rents that the city charged to shopkeepers contributed to the public coffers.

The arrangements of the Classical period (5th–4th centuries B.C.) were less imposing, but there is no doubt that buying and selling had a long history in and around the public square. Writers of the 4th century B.C. tell us that a wide variety of goods were hawked from temporary structures – tables, wicker booths, and the like – set up within and on the fringes of the square, and the practice undoubtedly goes back to earlier times. These authors also make it clear that the neighborhoods immediately adjacent to the Agora were packed with more permanent commercial establishments. Here, in buildings of various forms, goods were both sold and manufactured. Commodities attested by the ancient writers include meat, sausages, fish, vegetables, fruit, nuts, barley groats, bread, wine, wreaths, ribbons, slaves, pottery, items made of bronze and leather, figurines, and books. You could also find moneylenders and barbers near the Agora. Shops offering the same commodity were clustered together, and these concentrations served ancient Athenians as landmarks: when the comic poet Menander (4th century B.C.) wrote, «Wait for me at the olive oil», everyone knew what he meant.

We are not so lucky today, but over the years considerable evidence about the commercial activities of the city has come to light. Beginning in the 1970s, the excavation of substantial commercial buildings outside the northern and eastern sides of the square has focused attention on this aspect of the space, encouraging a review of objects and structures found much earlier in the project.

Identifying Commercial Buildings

Sometimes we can pinpoint the location of particular merchants by studying the broken and discarded objects they left behind. Thus, a heavy concentration of large clay amphoras (vessels designed for the long-distance shipping of liquids, which are described in more detail by Mark Lawall in Chapter 5) spread over a large area just outside the southeast corner of the square tells us that wine importers did business there in the 5th century B.C. Nearby, a similar collection of perfume bottles, thrown into wells and cisterns of the 5th to the 2nd century B.C., reveals that here was the perfume market, described by the 5th-century comic poet Aristophanes as the haunt of gossips and feckless young men.

A more concrete picture emerges from the remains of Classical buildings that clearly served commercial purposes: places not only where objects were sold but also where they were manufactured. Without exception, and as we would expect, these lay outside the Agora proper, but often as close to it as the builders could manage. They are nestled among dwellings, and some are indistinguishable from private houses in their plans. In these cases, the owner or tenant simply devoted part of his living space to his profession. For example, a hearth and deposits of marble and metal waste show that craftsmen worked in house D, a dwelling located along a road running south from the southwest corner of the square (Fig. 39 #10). In the larger house C, next door and to the south and, in one phase of its history, connected by a door to house D, an isolated room opens directly onto the street and probably served as a shop, where items manufactured inside were offered to the public. In another house, part of a block of dwellings just to the south of the public square (Fig. 39 #9), large containers (pithoi) set into a plastered floor bear witness to industrial or commercial activity (dyeing? felting? laundering?), while the profits are attested by the many lost coins – including two rare silver ones – discovered in the successive floor levels of one of the house's rooms. The same cheek-by-jowl arrangement of living and working space is evoked in a 4th-century B.C. Athenian inscription found at the Agora (I 1749), describing property confiscated from Philokrates of Hagnous, a prominent citizen who, indicted for treason by his political enemies, had left town rather than stand trial. The accused had owned two workshops (ergostasia), bounded on the north and east by two houses (also his property), on the west by a workshop owned by someone else, and on the south by a road leading to the square.

The North Side of the Agora

⇨ Fig. 39
Plan of the Agora before the erection of the Stoa of Attalos in the middle of the 2nd century B.C. Buildings specifically designed for commercial and industrial activity are shaded. Numbers are referred to in the text.

Beginning just after the Persian Wars of the 480s, Athenians began to erect buildings that were specifically designed for use as shops and workshops. We can point to more than a half dozen structures, located at practically every entrance to the Agora, that share a common plan. The recurrent, identifying feature is a row of rooms of uniform size, much like the row of shops behind the colonnade of the Stoa of Attalos, but – as we shall see – there is considerable variety in the pattern.

The simplest form is illustrated by a building north of the Agora (Fig. 39 #1), right behind a large stoa that faced onto the public square and is probably to be identified as the Painted Stoa known from literary sources. The shop building has not yet been completely excavated, but as so far revealed, it has at least four rooms, side by side and opening onto a street at the west. Although its plan is simple, it was well constructed. The lower part of the south wall was built of fine limestone masonry, while elsewhere in the building polygonal masonry and rubble foundations preserve the floor plan. The upper walls were built of mud brick, a remarkably durable material when protected by a good roof.

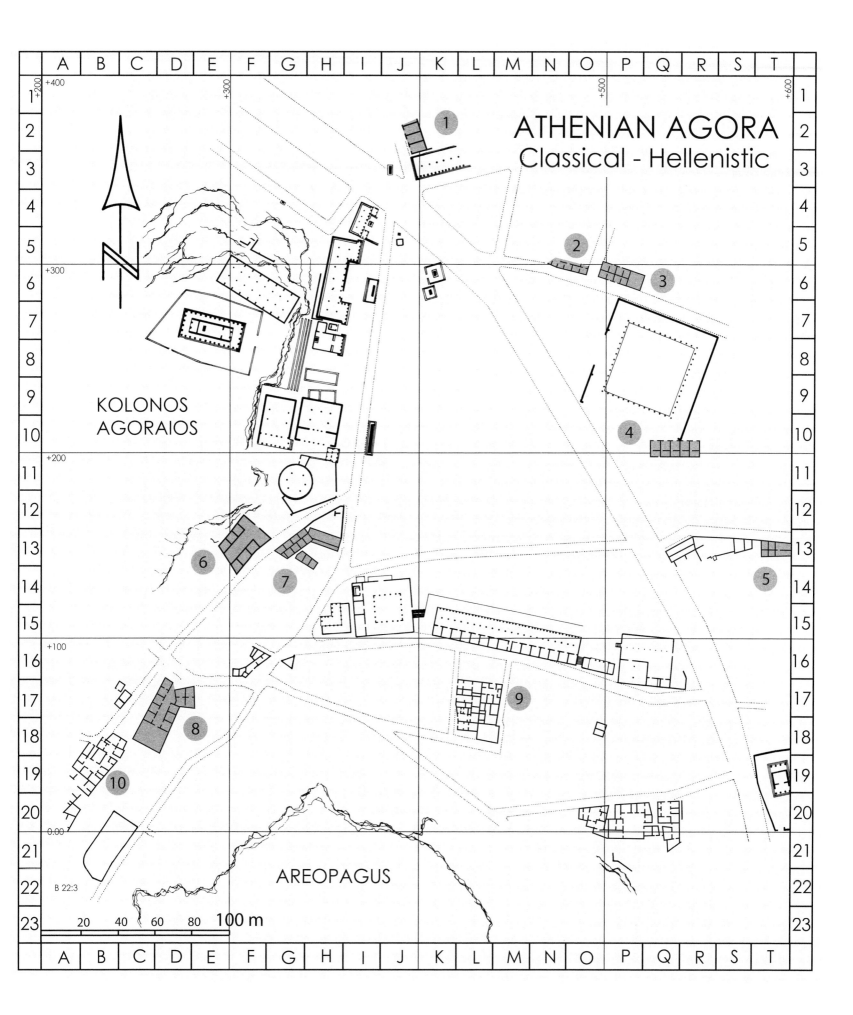

ATHENIAN AGORA
Classical - Hellenistic

KOLONOS
AGORAIOS

AREOPAGUS

B 22:3

20 40 60 80 100 m

Fig. 40
Clay impression of a
fragment from a large
bronze vessel (T 4461)
(with modern cast), found
in the commercial building
behind the Painted Stoa.
This provides evidence
that workers in metal were
among the tenants of the
building.

Fig. 41
Pyre in the southernmost
room of the commercial
building behind the Painted Stoa (pyre J 3:7; ca.
325 B.C.).

The building was erected close to the year 400 B.C. and was occupied for many centuries thereafter. In the manner typical of simple Classical buildings, floors were periodically replaced by bringing in and tamping down a thin layer of clay over the old, worn surface; small pieces of pottery inadvertently incorporated in the floor help date the sequence. Ten clay floors in the south room of our building record occupation down into the 1st century A.D. The building may have stood for as much as a millennium, until the Slavic invasions of the 6th century A.D., but we have only the rebuilt walls, not the floors, of that later phase.

The plan alone gives us a clue to the function of the building. It cannot be a dwelling, for its layout is utterly different from that of the Classical houses revealed by excavations around the Agora and elsewhere in Athens and the Greek world. Its location outside the square argues against an official, political function, and it certainly is not a shrine or a temple. Fortunately, the tenants were careless housekeepers, and abundant evidence of their activities has been found in the fabric of the floors. Shallow depressions contained iron and bronze slag and bronze filings; patches of pigment stained floor surfaces; and marble dust and chips and fragments of lead and pumice were embedded in the floors. A clay impression (Fig. 40) taken from a piece of bronze relief work, an artisan's record of an object to be recreated in the future, was found in the second room from the south. In the southernmost room, a Y-shaped clay drain had been installed to channel water from the floor out through the street door. From all this we can conclude that workers in metal and marble made up some of the tenants of the building, though other crafts that leave less durable testimony could also have been practiced here.

The floors also revealed intriguing evidence of these workers' religious practices: small collections of drinking cups, lamps, miniature saucers and cooking pots, and burned animal bones that had been buried beneath them in shallow pits (Figs. 41 and 42). The bones (primarily of sheep and goats) tell us that these are the remains of sacrifices, in which part of the victim was burned as an offering to the gods, as was the universal Greek custom. Several of these deposits were found in each room of our building, with the total number now standing at twelve. These so-called saucer pyres are a regular feature of private buildings around the fringes of the Agora square; more than 50 have come to light in the course of the excavations. Although the purpose of the sacrifices they document is unknown, saucer pyres are most commonly found in buildings that were devoted, at least in part, to craft and industry. A craftsman would have good reason to seek the favor of the gods. He needed their help to insure the success of the often complex and unpredictable industrial processes upon which his livelihood depended. His work could be dangerous, and he needed their protection to insure his personal safety. If the work went awry, or if he or his coworkers suffered an accident, he might need to avert malign influences by ritual means. Alternatively, sacrifices may have accompanied renovation of a space or a change of tenants. But whatever the reason, the association with craft activities is clear from the distribution of saucer pyres around the Agora.

Another shop building on the north side of the Agora illustrates a more complex version of the plan (Fig. 39 #3), where the row of rooms is doubled. Each row faces outward — on the south onto a street, on the north either onto a street or a courtyard — and there is a large courtyard at the building's eastern end. (A poorly preserved twin [Fig. 39 #2] stood just to its west). As in the simpler structure discussed above, the building was long-lived (from just after the Persian Wars of the 480s down to the early 2nd century A.D.), and here, too, saucer pyres were buried under the floors: three of them, dating in the 4th and 3rd centuries B.C.

There is little evidence for what went on here during the first 150 years of the building's history. Metal waste, tools, and molds, however, attest the presence of bronze-workers from the later 4th to the 2nd century B.C., replaced in one shop by masons in the later 3rd and 2nd centuries B.C. High concentrations of bronze coins reflect commercial activity, and a deposit of 3rd-century B.C. amphoras in one shop points to a merchant in wine and foodstuffs. Thus there is evidence of a variety of operations, industrial and commercial, side by side and changing through time. Precisely the same picture of changing tenantry is painted by the 4th-century B.C. orator Aeschines, in his speech against Timarchos (1.124):

If a physician moves into one of these shops on the street, it is called a clinic. But if he moves out and a smith moves into this same shop, it is called a smithy; if a fuller moves in, a laundry; if a carpenter, a carpentry-shop; and if a pimp and his whores move in, we call it a brothel.

The passage also points to challenges for the archaeologist. The activities of a smith may leave durable traces, a fuller's shop may be furnished with vats, and a carpenter may leave a trail of nails; but clinics and brothels are unlikely to leave evidence of their short occupation of rented quarters.

Fig. 42
Pottery from another pyre in the building (pyre J 2:9, in the third room from south; ca. 300 B.C.).

Other Shop Buildings around the Agora

Common sense tells us that a location near the public square, where citizens had occasion to go on a daily basis, would be advantageous for a small businessman; and, indeed, the orator Lysias, in a speech written around 400 B.C. in defense of a shopkeeper (24.20), observes that most customers frequent the shops nearest the Agora, many fewer those establishments that are farther away. If we look around the edges of the Agora, and especially at the points where roads enter the square, we find those shops. One of these lay along a road that led eastward toward the area that would later be occupied by the Roman Agora (Fig. 39 #5). Rich debris from its courtyard shows that in the 4th century B.C. workers in bone and horn and a maker of clay figurines shared these facilities with a butcher, a wine shop, and a tavern. Another shop building stood on the site of the later Stoa of Attalos (Fig. 39 #4) in the second quarter of the 2nd century B.C.; here a larger front room was paired with a smaller back room — shop and storeroom? Tavern and service area? Debris outside and behind the building

Fig. 43
Aerial view of the Poros Building, so named for the large limestone blocks that were used within its walls.

testifies to occupancy by metalworkers and another tavern. And just outside the southwestern corner of the square, three shop buildings are arranged around an open area (Fig. 39 #7), their sequential occupancy spanning the years from the 5th to the early 1st century B.C.

A road leads southward from this complex into the heart of an industrial neighborhood. Rodney Young, excavating here in the late 1940s, found so much marble waste that he dubbed this thoroughfare «the Street of the Marble Workers». It leads down to houses C and D (Fig. 39 #10), mentioned earlier as the workplaces of marble- and metal-workers, and on the way it passes another building that we might add to our collection of shops: the Poros Building (Fig. 39 #8; Fig. 43), so named for the large limestone blocks that were used in its walls. Margaret Crosby, who carried out excavations here from 1947 to 1950, filled more than 15 notebooks with observations of this building. A generation later, John Camp devoted another season to further work here. Even so, the Poros Building remains something of a mystery.

Sections of wall and cuttings in bedrock make the plan clear: two rows of same-sized rooms and a courtyard, like the more complex shop building plan discussed earlier. Here, however, the rooms probably turn inward on an unroofed corridor (though we cannot be sure; long stretches of the western wall are missing, and some rooms may have had doors opening to the street). Four rooms at the northeast have a different orientation and may belong to a different structure. The building was constructed around the middle of the 5th century B.C., and debris and fallen roof tiles show that it was badly damaged around the end of that century. Remodeled sometime thereafter, it probably survived until the 1st century B.C., when it was utterly destroyed by the soldiers of the Roman general Sulla, who sacked the city of Athens in 86 B.C.

Although its plan and history are now known, the function of the Poros Building has never been established with certainty. The same-sized rooms have suggested to some that it might be an apartment building, but the lack of a water supply in its first phase would have made these spaces unappealing as living quarters. The large size and good construction shows that its builders had considerable resources; was the Poros Building built by the Athenian state to serve some official purpose? It is unlikely to have been a law court: its courtyard is too small for most Athenian juries and its small rooms unsuited to Athenian legal activities. It may have served as offices for public officials, but what need did such functionaries have for a large courtyard? Ingenious but ultimately unconvincing arguments have been deployed to identify it as the state prison – a structure most vividly known from Plato's account of the death of Sokrates. It is Athenian shop buildings, however, that furnish the closest parallels to its plan, and heavy deposits of marble chips and dust show that masons worked in the northern part of the building in the late 5th and 4th centuries B.C. Other remnants of industrial activity include a basin, an enormous jar (*pithos*) and an amphora sunk into the floor of the northwestern room (Fig. 44); a deposit of bronze-casting molds in fill of the second half of the 4th century B.C., just north of the entrance to the building; and massive amounts of slag in the destruction debris over the building's northeastern parts. Furthermore, at least three saucer

pyres were buried under its floors in the course of the 4th century B.C. It may be, then, that the Poros Building was built to provide working space for artisans and shopkeepers; if, as its substantial construction suggests, it was built at public expense, it may be a forerunner of the Stoa of Attalos, bringing in income for the state in the form of rents.

Fig. 44
Industrial installations in the northwest room of the Poros Building. The industrial character of these discoveries suggests that the building served as a working space for artisans.

The Strategeion (?)

A very poorly preserved building located on the same street, farther to the north and closer to the square (Fig. 39 #6) also poses a puzzle. It too included large limestone blocks in its walls, and, as far as its disturbed state allows one to judge, its plan was not unlike that of the Poros Building, with which it is about contemporary. Its footprint is an irregular square, with a courtyard at the north and perhaps two rows of rooms and a corridor at the south. As with the Poros Building, size and construction hint at public sponsorship; not only does its fabric include some large poros blocks, but a very considerable amount of bedrock was cut away to make a level space for its construction. The building is labeled «Strategeion?» – Office of the Generals – on plans of the Agora. Literary sources

tell us that the 10 generals of Athens had offices in a building of that name, and it was probably located in or near the public square. Fragments of at least four inscriptions that once stood in front of the Strategeion have been found on the west side of the square, hinting that the office was in this general region. This is the sum of the evidence; we know nothing about the likely plan of such a building, except that it had to provide space for 10 generals and at least sometimes for the storage of military equipment.

Unfortunately, even the lowest floors of the building are missing, robbing us of potential clues to its function. Two fascinating things have come to light below the level of those floors, however. In 1935 Rodney Young discovered a small saucer pyre

that had been buried there in the 3rd century B.C., remnants of the ritual so frequently associated with workshops — and never, so far, attested in Athenian public buildings. Seventy years later, in the summer of 2005, a spectacular hoard of about 400 silver coins (Figs. 45 and 46) was found just centimeters below the level at which the earlier excavations had stopped. Whoever occupied the building had occasion to deal in large sums of money, but we do not know whether these were public or private funds, or whether the person who buried them was a general, a banker, or a thief — or all three. But searching for parallels elsewhere, we may recall that scattered coins — and even silver ones — are regularly found in the floors of commercial buildings and houses where crafts were practiced. Excavation continues in the building; during the last days of the 2006 season large deposits of marble chips began to appear, adding another piece of evidence for the presence of craftsmen here. A more detailed description of the coin hoard by Agora conservator Amandina Anastassiades is provided in Chapter 9.

Through the work of the excavations some meat has been put on the bones of ancient descriptions, and we can better visualize the workplaces crowded around the public square of Athens. Imagine walls rising from the recovered foundations; add the rhythmic clink of the mason's mallet, the cries of vendors, the pungent smell of the smith's charcoal fire and the dyer's vat, and the bustle of customers and craftsmen in the narrow streets leading to and from the square — and you can recover a small but spicy slice of ancient Athenian life.

Fig. 45 (above)

Hoard of about 400 silver coins emerging from the earth in the «Strategeion», the building sometimes identified as the Office of the Generals.

Fig. 46
Detail of the coin hoard.

Living Near the Agora: Houses and Households in Central Athens

by Barbara Tsakirgis

Numerous private houses and structures that combined both residential and commercial activity, as Susan Rotroff discusses in Chapter 2, have come to light around the periphery of the Athenian Agora. Some of the residential areas define the edge of the civic space and others are on the slopes of the surrounding hills. Houses appear in the Athenian Agora from the inception of its identity as a civic space in the Late Archaic period, and they count among the last of the buildings to be constructed here. Large houses from even the Late Roman period have been excavated on the north slope of the Areopagus. Although much interesting information has been uncovered about Hellenistic, Roman, and Byzantine domestic life, this chapter will focus on the earlier houses of the later Archaic and Classical periods (6th to 4th centuries B.C.) in order to review the excavated remains and to introduce some of the recent approaches to the buildings and their contents.

The area delimited by the Areopagus to the south, the Kolonos Agoraios hill to the west, and the Eri-

danos River to the north may not have suggested itself to the earliest Athenians as a place for habitation. The abundance of water, rather than the lack of it, probably deterred the Athenians of the Neolithic period from building their homes at the foot of the hills or near the river. Domestic wells clustered on the northwest shoulder of the Acropolis show that the inhabitants of Neolithic Athens preferred a more defensible and well-drained location for their homes, high up near the Acropolis springs. In the course of his excavation of the houses in the valley bordered by the Pnyx and Areopagus hills, Rodney Young dug through 14 meters of fill that had accumulated after the destruction of the Great Drain (built in the 6th century B.C. to dispose of surface water) and its Roman successor. That fill demonstrates that any houses built in the low-lying areas before the creation of the Great Drain would have been threatened with a similar depth of silt and pebbles that washed off the rocky slopes of the surrounding hills.

The Archaic Period

Literary and archaeological evidence places the center of Archaic Athens elsewhere than at the site of the Classical Agora. Thucydides famously locates older Athens to the south of the Acropolis and excavations and recent research confirm the historian's statement. In his examination of the Early Iron

Age remains in the area that later became the Classical Agora, John Papadopoulos examined numerous wells and their associated deposits and proposed that the Late Geometric and Proto-Attic buildings (late 8th through 7th centuries B.C.) were not primarily residential in nature. Rather, although some

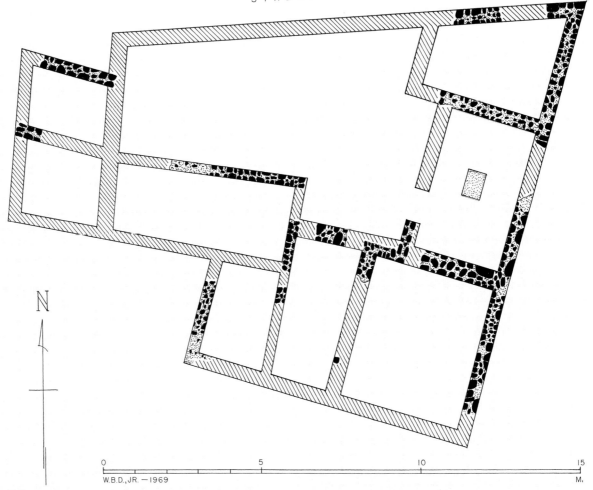

N

0   5   10   15

W.B.D.,JR. — 1969   M.

Fig. 47
Restored plan of early 5th-
century B.C. Greek house
in section Omega.

may have been lived in by shop slaves, most were workshops for craftsmen who toiled in the potters' quarter here. Thus, although we can say that there was Early Iron Age habitation in the area that later became the Classical Agora, the space was not really a dedicated residential area at that time. Because the Early Iron Age wells and their deposits that provide evidence from this period have essentially no associated architectural remains, we have no idea of the plans of the putative potters' shops.

The evidence for domestic architecture in this part of Athens increases in the 6th century B.C., and by 500 B.C. there are traces of houses built around, but not in, what was becoming the public heart of Athens. A better understanding of the history of habitation in this part of Athens will ultimately help us fully identify the process by which and the period during which the area was converted from a potter's field to a civic center; current theories date

that transition to the later 6th and earliest 5th centuries B.C. In their locations, the 6th century B.C. houses appear to respect most of the area that would later become the public space, and that avoidance by house builders of what will become the central floor of the Agora suggests one of three possibilities: perhaps the low-lying territory was subject to the inconvenient and insalubrious runoff of water from the hills, as suggested earlier, or it was already designated public space, or it was simply unattractive as a location for house building because most civic life in Archaic Athens was still taking place on the other side of the Acropolis.

Houses in central Athens in the late 6th and early 5th centuries B.C. already display some of the features that would become part of the typical residence of the Classical period. The Late Archaic house under the northwest corner of the Classical block on the north slope of the Areopagus and another under the Late Roman house in excavation area Omega (Fig. 47) are the most completely excavated examples of Archaic residences around the Agora. There appears to be neither a regular plan for the houses nor a common size. The acute angles seen at the corners of some of the houses imply a preexisting street system – not an orthogonal grid but rather a collection of thoroughfares established during the long history of earlier human habitation in this part of Athens. An unroofed area is part of the domestic space. It is usually centrally located or sometimes to the south of major rooms, as in a partially excavated house north of the Eridanos River. There are no formal pavements or wall paintings, and no traces of either pillars or columns designed to serve as supports for a portico exist in the Archaic domestic courtyards. All of the architectural remains are modest in scale, materials, and decor, and they contrast by the end of the 6th century B.C. with the emerging Athenian interest in building public structures at large scale and of cut stone blocks.

The Classical Period

In the late 6th and early 5th centuries B.C., some of the earlier houses were demolished and built over to make way for public structures. This transition is best seen in the houses that precede the City Eleusinion, the sanctuary of Demeter situated on the north slope of the Areopagus. Margaret Miles has dated the demolition of these modest dwellings to the late 6th century B.C., precisely when John Camp and others have recognized the transition of the area from private holdings to public space. A more certain force for change in the city's architectural landscape was the Persian invasion of 480/79 B.C. The *barbaroi* cut a swath through this section of Athens, an area perhaps already emerging as the civic center and certainly already bisected by the Panathenaic Way. T. Leslie Shear Jr. examined the material deposited in wells in and near the Agora after the cleanup of the Persian attack, and, in addition to confirming that the debris dates to 480 B.C., he has shown that the assembled pottery stemmed from a variety of sources, including domestic activity. The sherds of household pottery are one more piece of evidence for habitation in the area before 480 B.C. The importance of the «Persian destruction deposits»

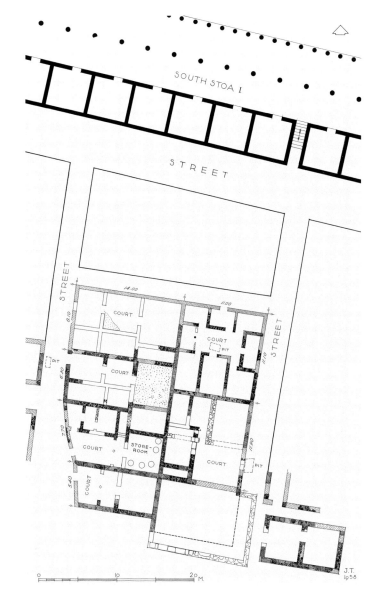

Fig. 48
Plan showing a block of Classical houses on the north slope of the Areopagus (post 480 B.C.).

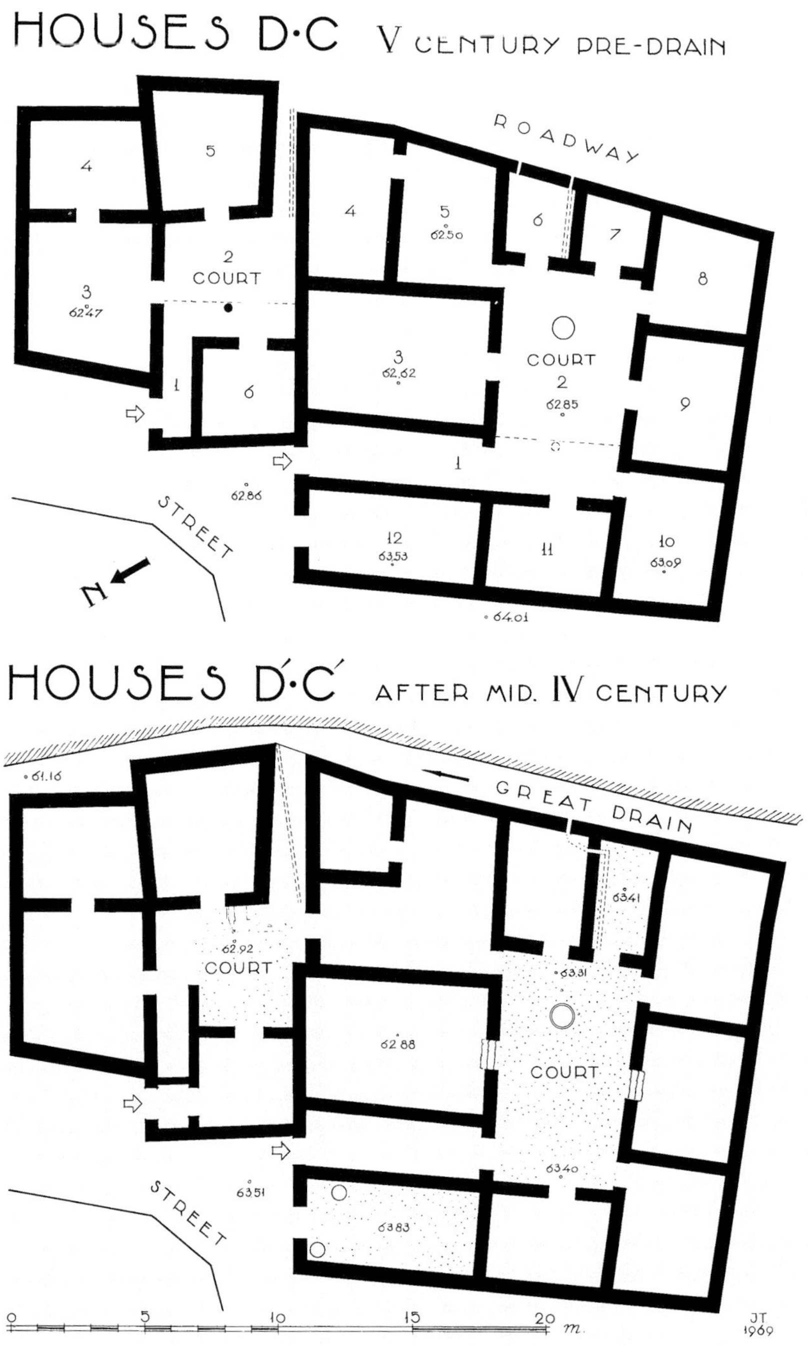

Fig. 49
Houses C and D in the
industrial district. The plans
show the layout of these
houses in the 5th and 4th
centuries B.C.

for ceramic research is discussed by Kathleen Lynch in Chapter 6.

Houses multiply in central Athens after the post-Persian cleanup. Many were built shortly after 479 B.C., others as late as 460 B.C. The new residential structures line the preexisting streets and have the same irregular footprints their predecessors had. Nowhere do we find evidence of an orthogonal grid of streets, nowhere the regular type of houses found in colonial sites or refoundations such as the city of Olynthos in northern Greece. Acute angles in the plans abound and the classical Athenians must have had many headaches and many leaks as they roofed these dwellings lacking in right angles.

The Athenian houses of the Classical period, though not identical repetitions of the same plan, do share common features (Fig. 48). Unroofed courtyards, with an occasional covered portico on one side, lie at the center of the dwellings. More common in houses of the Classical period than before, but still not ubiquitous, are vestibules that served as buffers between the hubbub of city streets and the privacy within the home; this entry room can be recognized in the neighboring houses C and D in the so-called industrial district (Fig. 49), already mentioned by Susan Rotroff in Chapter 2. The street entrances to the vestibules are aligned at right angles to the doorway into the domestic courts, thus ensuring that someone standing at the street door would not be able to look directly into the courtyard, and thus into the heart of domestic life. This plan for controlled physical and visual access to the interior of the houses has been seen as a means of ensuring the privacy of the home and of the residents within, and would have been reinforced with wooden doors and curtains drawn across the entrances of rooms.

Luxurious internal appointments are scarce in Athenian houses of the Classical period. Recognizable dining rooms (*andrones*) are absent from most of the homes around the Agora; one in a house in excavation area Omega on the north slope of the Areopagus is the exception. Its square plan with a raised platform for the dining couches is very like the contemporaneous andrones seen in the houses at the northern site of Olynthos. Like those dining rooms, the Athenian example sported a pebble mosaic floor, here depicting fish, poorly preserved. Such an architecturally distinct and thus functionally limited room with raised platforms for couches was not necessary to the success of a drinking party (symposium) in 5th-century B.C. Athens and took up space that could be used otherwise in the small Classical houses. As long as sufficient couches were arranged in any given room when the time came the symposium could occur, whether the room was square or not. Little evidence exists in Classical Athenian houses for painted walls and mosaic

HOUSES D·C V CENTURY PRE-DRAIN

HOUSES D·C′ AFTER MID. IV CENTURY

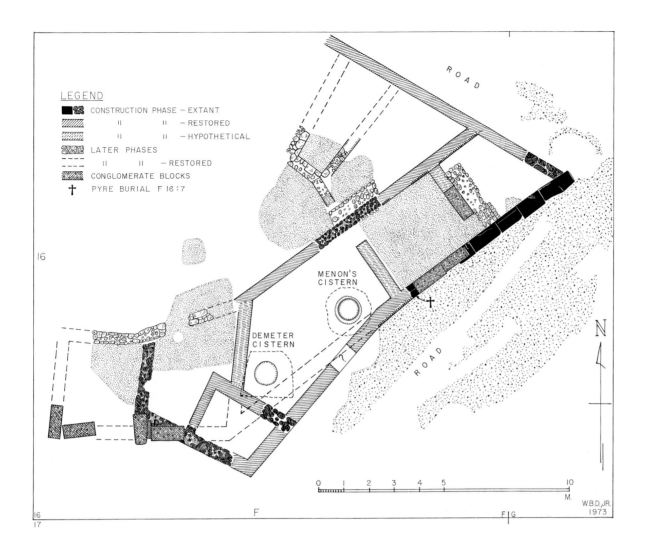

LEGEND
CONSTRUCTION PHASE — EXTANT
" " — RESTORED
" " — HYPOTHETICAL
LATER PHASES
" " — RESTORED
CONGLOMERATE BLOCKS
† PYRE BURIAL F 16:7

ROAD

MENON'S CISTERN

DEMETER CISTERN

ROAD

N

0 1 2 3 4 5 10
M.

W.B.D.,JR.
1973

16

16
17

F

F G

Fig. 50
Plan of the house of
Mikion and Menon, two
marble-workers. As the
shaded areas show, there
were multiple construction
phases in many Athenian
houses.

floors, as are found in the contemporaneous houses at Olynthos. Only the mosaic mentioned above and another of chipped stones set in a geometric pattern in another room of the same house are reminiscent of the more elaborate floors with mythological scenes found in the northern town.

The houses built near the Agora in the mid-5th century B.C. were lived in for a long time. Almost 200 years passed between the construction of the house of Mikion and Menon (Fig. 50) ca. 460 B.C. and its final use ca. 275 B.C. Houses C and D in the industrial district were inhabited for an even longer period. The buildings of course experienced changes over time. Each generation had requirements that were different from those of its predecessors, and additions to the original space and alterations were made accordingly. Thus houses C and D, originally two separate dwellings, were combined in the 4th

century B.C. into one larger house whose northern section was given over in part to metalworking and whose southern section continued to be used as a residence.

Given the considerable traces of industrial activity present in the Classical houses in central Athens, it is reasonable to ask who their owners and/or residents may have been. Unfortunately, prosopographical evidence is wanting in most of the houses. Only a few *horoi* (inscribed stones indicating that a house was mortgaged), found in or built into houses, can be used to name some owners. The nomenclature suggests Athenians, and there is a possibility that some of the residents were resident aliens (*metics*) who rented the buildings from Athenian landlords — only a few resident foreigners were allowed the right to own property (*enktesis*) in Athens. If metics lived in some of the houses, their domestic assemblages of pots and dishes and other objects may reflect non-Athenian cultural or social practice, but as the buildings were constructed for Athenians, the overall layout of the houses probably reflects Athenian tastes and conduct. Our sources tell us that many metics lived in Melite and Kollytos, precisely the neighborhoods where houses have been excavated to the west and southwest of the Agora.

Understanding Domestic Space

Early research on the houses around the Agora emphasized architectural forms and discussed how house plans in the Agora compared with those of Classical houses found elsewhere. Recent research on houses has focused instead on the character of the household and the social life of the inhabitants of the buildings. In particular, scholars have attempted to reconstruct behavioral patterns based on the architecture as well as the attendant small finds. To that end, newer work on the Athenian houses has included a close study of the context material that can provide insight into the social history of the buildings. For example, research has focused on what we can learn from the Athenian

houses about the lives of women, the practice of domestic religion, and the use of some houses as combinations of living and working space.

Researchers studying Greek houses and households outside of Athens have recently examined the domestic assemblages and their distribution throughout the buildings. An important study of the houses at Olynthos proves that the small finds reveal much more than do the ground plans alone about daily life in the Classical dwellings. One serious impediment to a study of the Athenian houses and their domestic assemblages following the same approach is the simple fact that Athens rose again after each disaster. The residents cleaned up the mess resulting from the Persian sack, the attack by Sulla, and numerous natural calamities that damaged the city. Thus very little material in the houses around the Agora was found where it was used in the life of the home, in the context of its primary deposition. Much was recovered from where it was later discarded in building trenches, landfill, and cistern deposits.

The «place» of women in the Greek house has attracted considerable recent attention. Although some ancient Athenian sources such as Xenophon's *Oeconomicus* have been read to suggest that women were sequestered in a women's quarter (*gynaikōn*), scholars have recently rejected this idea and have proposed that women occupied most of, if not the whole, house. Perhaps, at certain times of the day, women might move from cooking in the courtyard and weaving in rooms lit from unroofed space to more secluded spaces in order to be away from the eyes of visiting strangers, but they probably normally worked and lived in even the most central and public parts of the house. The finds from the Athenian houses seem to confirm this theory,

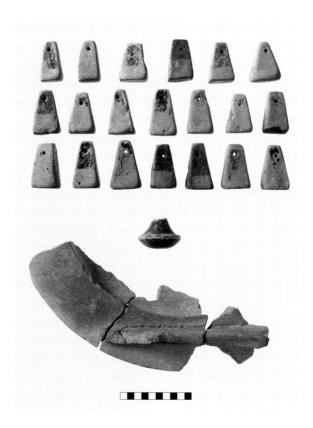

Fig. 51
Loomweights, a spindle whorl, and a brazier fragment from house C in the industrial district.

as there is little evidence for areas in which women might be sequestered, and the evidence suggests that women lived throughout the house. Clusters of objects associated with women's work have been found in many different areas, such as a group of loom weights, spindle whorl, and brazier from one room directly off the courtyard in house C in the industrial district (Fig. 51). The tools represent the spinning of thread and the weaving of cloth, and the brazier may have been used for heating the room or the dye to color the thread or cloth.

Just as the modest forms of houses caused them to be neglected by early excavators in favor of public architecture, buildings housing both residential and industrial activities were passed over in favor of those with recognizable *andrones* and more impressive interior decoration. Many of the Athenian houses around the Agora were occupied by workmen who left behind the detritus of their crafts. The hobnails and bone eyelets from the house of Simon (Fig. 52) are well-known debris from one craftsman's home and shop, made famous by the use of Sokrates and his younger pupils, but some remains from the house of Mikion and Menon deserve even greater attention. This family of sculptors worked and lived in a house just a block away from the southwest entrance of the Agora. None of their iron chisels remain, but they left behind both unfinished stone sculpture, including a votive to the Mother of the Gods, and a few of their tools, a stone pounder or polisher, a pumice smoother, and several lead pencils (Fig. 53). The stone masons used the central court as house entrance, workshop, and possibly also showroom. Chips and dust from the marble carpeted the central space that would have provided light, air, and access to the surrounding working and living rooms of the house.

Fig. 52
Plan of the house of Simon. The hobnails and bone eyelets found here show that this was both house and workplace for a shoe-maker. The house of Simon was also one of the places where Sokrates met those of his pupils too young to enter the Athenian Agora (note its relationship to the boundary stone), yet more evidence of the multiple functions of Athenian houses.

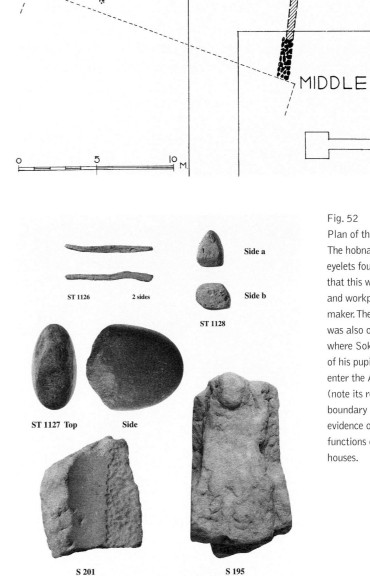

⇨ Fig. 53
Sculptor's tools and unfinished sculpture from the house of Mikion and Menon. This family of sculptors worked and lived in a house just a block away from the southwest entrance of the Agora.

Religion in the Household

Fig. 54
Relief herm carved on the
jamb of a shop in the Stoa
of Attalos. It is likely that
humble wooden or relief
herms such as this served to
mark the boundary between
public and private spaces.

Every aspect of Athenian life was imbued with religion, and the household was no exception. Literature speaks of ritual practice in the house on a regular basis before meals and symposia, as well as to mark the significant events of life — birth, marriage, and death. Many of these religious observations, marked by ephemeral prayers and plant material, left no trace in the archaeological record. The household hearth, locus and focus of these events, is also surprisingly difficult to identify in excavated Athenian houses, despite its attested importance in literary sources: we know that a father carried his newborn child around the hearth in the rite of *amphidromia* in order to mark its acceptance into the family; the wedding banquet was held here and the new bride was welcomed into her husband's home at his family's hearth; the deceased was remembered at a meal eaten beside it. But, despite the important role of this fireplace in the rites of passage and as the seat of household religion, only one hearth has been found in an Archaic or Classical house around the Agora. Perhaps, as Michael Jameson proposed, the humble terracotta brazier served as a portable hearth for ritual as well as for a source of heat and a cooking stove. It was therefore an object of changeable identity suitable for a flexible use of space in the house.

Equally absent in the archaeological record are the «herms» said to have stood outside the street doors of Athenian homes, which are discussed by John Camp in Chapter 1. These household sentinel posts, topped with a head of Hermes, marked the boundary between public and private and are famous for having been attacked by a band of drunken revelers on the eve of the Sicilian expedition in 415 B.C. It is likely that in a domestic setting humble wooden or relief herms, like that carved on the jamb of a shop in the Stoa of Attalos (Fig. 54), served just as well as the grander stone versions erected in some public areas to mark the boundary between public and private.

Past research on Athenian houses has served as a stepping-stone for the present, allowing us to go beyond the simple architecture and to take into consideration all of the finds. Athenian houses can now be understood in the broader context of the development of the city of Athens and in the social history of the Archaic and Classical city-state.

Roman Portraits from the Athenian Agora: Recent Finds

by Lee Ann Riccardi

Any study of the Roman portraits that have been found recently in the Athenian Agora rests on the pioneering work done by Evelyn B. Harrison, the author of the very first excavation monograph, *Portrait Sculpture* (*Athenian Agora* I, 1953), published by the American School to report on the Agora excavations. Harrison's analysis of stylistic traits, tools, and techniques created a framework on which other scholars could build, and her research established a typological and chronological basis for analysis that has been adopted and refined by many others. Although in her later work she focused on Greek material rather than Roman portraiture, she has continued to publish Agora sculpture and is one of the many scholars whose career began with, and has been shaped by, her work in the Agora.

The five Roman portraits presented here consist of three female heads and two male heads. Although these pieces constitute just a small sample of the many sculptures that must have crowded the Roman Agora and its Archaic, Classical, and Hellenistic predecessors, a detailed examination reveals the rich array of information that can be gained from close analysis.

The Female Portraits

The three female heads, different in date and found in different secondary contexts, exhibit some basic similarities that allow them to be discussed together. All were portraits of aristocratic women, probably benefactors or the relatives of benefactors of the city of Athens, and their original display in the public space of the Agora would most likely have been in recognition of some generous service or donation to Athens. The portraits were found in Byzantine levels of the Agora excavations, two of them used as building material in medieval constructions and the third thrown into an abandoned storage jar (*pithos*).

Their hairstyles allow the dates of their initial creations to be determined with some certainty. One is from the late first or early second quarter of the 2nd century A.D., one from the last quarter of the 2nd century A.D., and one from the 3rd century A.D.

The earliest portrait (S 2303), a life-size image of an unknown woman, was found in a *pithos* in mixed 12th- to 13th-century medieval fill (Fig. 55). It was found in 1970. Although an exact parallel for the hairstyle cannot be found, it is clear that it is a variant of the styles popular in aristocratic Roman circles in late Trajanic or early Hadrianic times, that is sometime in the late first or early second quarter of the 2nd century A.D. The hairstyle displays a complicated configuration of a series of braids swept up tightly from the neck and wrapped around the head. The hair in the front around the face is crimped loosely into waves rather than drawn into a complex «tower» normally worn by ladies of the early Trajanic period, and the braids are wrapped around the entire circumference of the head rather than pulled into a bun at the top as in late Hadrianic or early Antonine portraits.

Fig. 55
Female portrait, second quarter of the 2nd century A.D. (S 2303): frontal view, rear view, and left profile.

Fig. 56
Female portrait, last quarter of the 2nd century A.D. (S 3423): frontal view, rear view, and left profile.

Fig. 57
Female portrait, third quarter of the 3rd century A.D. (S 3425): frontal view, rear view, and left profile.

The second female portrait (S 3423) dates to late Antonine or early Severan times, the last quarter of the 2nd century A.D., and was found in 1992 (Fig. 56). It was built into a Byzantine wall dating to the 9th or 10th century, its eyes scratched out and the head turned upside down. This hairstyle presents a fairly close parallel to others from the late Antonine or early Severan eras. Details such as curls escaping on the side of the neck, perhaps meant to suggest a wig, are common in this era, and the large size of the bun and the nature of the interwoven strands can be paralleled in other female hairstyles of the period.

The final female portrait (S 3425) is a badly weathered head found in 1993 built into a Byzantine rubble buttress (Fig. 57). It too was found upside down. Although the specific details of the hairstyle are impossible to determine, parallels for the general outlines of the coiffure are seen in female hairstyles from the third quarter of the 3rd century. The long hair is divided into a series of braids and then pulled up and attached to the top of the head.

Christian Treatment of Ancient Statuary

In Christian times, Roman statuary was highly charged material. Heads such as these were not just convenient blocks of *spolia* available for reuse. Many literary sources attest that to many of the Christian faithful, sculptures, especially heads, were considered to be infused with pagan associations and had a dark religious power. The spirit of anthropomorphic images was both feared and respected by Early Christian iconoclasts, and examples of attempts to neutralize that power abound. The Agora heads were used in medieval contexts in ways that would be most likely to diffuse this religious energy — that is, with their eyes scratched out and other facial features destroyed, and with the heads inserted into constructions upside down and facing down or inward, or, in the case of the head from earlier in the 2nd century, hidden in an out-of-use *pithos*.

Defacement and concealment of pagan images by Christians was not unusual in various parts of the Roman Empire, including Greece. Desecrating facial features (especially eyes), beheading, gouging, and amputating various limbs were the most common behaviors. After mutilation, the offend-ing sculpture might be consigned to the underworld by being buried or thrown into a river or a well. A dramatic example of statue desecration is seen in a medallion portrait of Alexander from Aphrodisias. Its face was deliberately hammered and a deep incision carved across the throat, probably an attempt to decapitate the image (as suggested by the excavator, R. R. R. Smith). Several examples of attempts to destroy the power of pagan sculptures have been found in the Agora excavations, including a relief depicting nymphs and deities in the Cave of Pan, which was turned upside-down and reused as a step block in a Late Roman villa after all the heads of the figures had been deliberately hacked away. Another example can be seen in a relief of Artemis, found in the bottom of a well, which is in virtually pristine condition except that the face of the goddess was knocked off.

These female portraits, then, provide information not only about the eras in which they were created but also about the eras in which they were reused, and they demonstrate that pagan portraits continued to evoke distrust and fear well into the medieval era.

Portrait of a Man Wearing a Bust-Crown

The male heads were both found in the summer of 2002. The earlier and more elaborate of them (S 3500) comes from mixed fill in the vicinity of the City Eleusinion (Fig. 58). It is a slightly larger than life-size early 3rd-century A.D. head of a man wearing a crown bearing eight small busts. This type of crown is known from ancient literature, inscriptions, coins, mosaics, and sculptures. Of the more than 20 known examples of sculpted portraits wearing these crowns, no others have a certain provenance from Greece.

The head itself is a portrait of a bearded man with thick curly hair. It is broken irregularly at the neck in such a way that its original context cannot be determined. Because the top of the head is much less detailed than the rest, however, and the back of the crown only roughly finished, it is clear that the sculptor expected that these areas would be above the eye level of most viewers. The head, therefore, probably belonged to a statue or at least to a bust that would have been placed on a high base or herm pillar.

The most remarkable feature of the portrait is the crown, a headdress consisting of three parts. The lowest is a thin, undecorated round band, or *strophion*. The second tier of the crown consists of another thin round band, decorated with triple rows of overlapping tiny pointed single-lobed leaves, all directed toward the top of the head. This middle portion of the crown is carved in relatively flat relief and the leaves lack any sort of internal detail, but the small size and general shape suggest myrtle leaves. Finally, the upper portion of the crown consists of a flat narrow band at the back of the head, which widens abruptly above the ears to wrap around the front. Decorating this band are eight small busts executed in relief. The busts are not equally spaced around the head of the portrait, but rather are crowded a little to the right. This results in one of the busts being centered approximately over the bridge of the nose of the portrait.

The style of the hair is readily comparable to that in portraits from the last quarter of the 2nd century and first quarter of the 3rd century A.D., and can be closely paralleled in portraits of *kosmetai* (the officials who supervised young men's training for citizenship) from Athens of the same era, particularly in the short rows of locks directly over the forehead, the drilling by which each lock is disengaged from the others, and the channels in the locks that create pockets of light and shadow.

Further evidence for the date of the original carving of the portrait can be seen in the form and character of the bust-crown adorning the head. Crowns that are tripartite, consisting of a lower *strophion*, a decorative middle tier, and an upper tier with small busts directly attached appear to have been the style of the late 2nd and early 3rd centuries, consistent with the date of the hair.

The busts on the crown of the Agora portrait were each provided with individual characteristics. Although the faces are worn, it is clear from the shapes of the heads and the treatment of the facial features that they were not intended to be identical. The artist clearly intended to show them as specific people, and they were meant to be recognizable, despite their small format. All are male, and each is depicted wearing Roman military dress, although the details of the costumes vary.

The portrait in the center must be the reigning emperor, probably Caracalla, and the one to his right his father and predecessor in imperial office, Septimius Severus. Others cannot be precisely identified, but likely candidates are previous members of the Severan and Antonine dynasties.

In order to determine why a statue of a man wearing a bust-crown would have been erected in Athens, the most important piece of evidence comes from the city of Aezani in Phrygia. On a long marble block built into the side of the stadium in a highly visible location, an inscription honors Marcus Ulpius Appuleius Eurykles, a native son of the city of Aezani, who lived in the middle of the 2nd century A.D. and who distinguished himself by holding a number of different and important offices. The block functions essentially as Eurykles' cursus honorum. The title of each of seven different offices that had been held by Eurykles was inscribed within a clearly distinguishable and different type of wreath or crown, and most correspond to the type otherwise known to have been worn by the holder of that office. For example, for his role as a priest of Diony-

Fig. 58
Bust of man, early 3rd
century A.D. (S 3500):
frontal view, rear view,
right profile, left profile,
and details of the busts on
the crown.

sos, he wore an ivy wreath; for his role as *archiereus* (chief priest) of Asia at the temple in Pergamon, he wore a bust-crown with 10 busts. The office of Panhellene is inscribed in the center of a crown bearing two small busts. These have been identified as Hadrian and Antoninus Pius, the recently deified and reigning emperors at the time Eurykles served in this office. On this evidence, it is clear that at least some delegates to the Panhellenion were identified by bust-crowns bearing the images of reigning or deified emperors.

The Panhellenion and the Headdress of a Panhellene

Lack of other evidence to support this conclusion is likely due to the rarity of references to the institution of the Panhellenion in classical literature. Information about the Panhellenion has been pieced together almost entirely from epigraphical sources, many of them exceedingly fragmentary. What can be said about the Panhellenion is that it was an institution established during Hadrian's rule and that it met in Athens. Its purpose is not entirely clear, but some of its activities are known.

Many of the inscriptions that provide information about the Panhellenion come from the surviving statue bases of its delegates. The epigraphical evidence makes clear that Panhellenes could receive the honor of a public statue in Athens, even if they had no other ties to the city, in exchange for active service to the city. Some Panhellenes received Athenian citizenship and permanent residency status. Unfortunately, it is rarely possible to attach specific portraits to specific bases, so identifying these officials, and also their costumes and attributes, is extremely difficult.

The Panhellenion had a close connection with Eleusis, the home of the important sanctuary of Demeter located near the city of Athens. Some of the most sacred and secret rites in antiquity were celebrated there, rites so mysterious that it is still not clear exactly what they were. The sanctuary, though always closely connected to Athens, had, from about the 8th century B.C. onward, an almost Panhellenic character. Thousands would come to the site from all over the Greek world for the annual celebration of the mysteries, which seems to have included, among other things, a reenactment of the abduction of Persephone by Hades. Eleusis enjoyed continuing popularity well into the Roman era, and several emperors were inducted into its mysteries.

Athens was always responsible for administering Eleusis, and was so intimately connected with the rituals that the initial procession originated in the Athenian Agora. The complex known as the City Eleusinion was constructed on the northern slopes of the Acropolis to serve both as headquarters for the administrators of the sanctuary and as storage for sacred objects carried in the procession. Finds suggest that statues of important Athenians connected with Eleusis were erected in the vicinity.

Inscriptions found both in Athens and in Eleusis reveal some details of the relationship of the Panhellenion to Eleusis. The Panhellenes paid for some building construction and repairs at the sanctuary, and it appears that at times they may even have taken over the administration of the annual sacred rites.

The mysteries at Eleusis were celebrated by sacred officials who held various offices. Inscriptions testify to several ranks of priests and priestesses, and some of these are accompanied by sculptures in the round or in relief depicting these officials. The epigraphical and sculptural evidence is clear that the customary headdress for priestly officials at Eleusis was a myrtle crown, which they would receive at their installation and wear while performing their duties. In sculpture, this crown is normally represented as bipartite, the lower band or *strophion* tied around the head, the upper a myrtle wreath.

In antiquity, several types of leafy wreaths were associated with various offices or honors. Particular kinds of leaves had symbolic significance, and thus sculptors represented them clearly in order to ensure that the meaning was visible to the viewer. Wreaths meant to show myrtle depict tiny, single-lobed pointed leaves like those on the leafy part of the crown of the Agora portrait, so these, too, were intended to be recognized as myrtle. This particular choice was not accidental. A myrtle wreath was part of the headdress of the Panhellene, and thus demonstrated the close relationship between the Panhellenion and Eleusis.

The Agora portrait therefore probably represents a delegate to the Panhellenion who was responsible for some sort of benefaction to Eleusis or Athens that earned him the honor of a public statue. In addition, the statue was likely set up near the area of its findspot, the City Eleusinion.

Fig. 59
Male head, 3rd century
A.D. (S 3510).

The Head of a Barbarian

The other male head found in 2002 (S 3510) probably dates to the 3rd century A.D. (Fig. 59). It comes from mixed fill in a Late Roman building. It is somewhat smaller than life-size and rather crudely carved, attesting that the sculptor had little interest in delineating details or establishing individual characteristics. The proportions are long and narrow, and it is oddly asymmetrical. The hair and beard are thicker and fuller on the left side than on the right, and though there is liberal use of the drill on the right side and around the face, the left and back were carved only with a chisel. Although broken irregularly at the neck, it is clear that the head was twisted to the left. Because of its long hair and slightly shaggy appearance, it could be a representation of a hero or a river god, but the diadem on the head makes it more likely to be a barbarian chieftain. Because of the oddly skewed proportions and appearance, it must not have been intended to stand alone or be seen frontally. Its ideal position would have been tilted to its left. Perhaps, then, it was part of a larger group, possibly also including a Roman emperor along the lines of the portrait of Hadrian from Ierapetra in Crete, now in Istanbul, or another

from the Library of Pantainos in the Agora (S 2518 shown in Fig. 60), which represents an emperor with a barbarian crouching at his feet. The crudity of the carving suggests the idea that the head was not the primary focus of the group, but rather played a supporting role in a larger piece of imperial propaganda. Although its original location in the Agora is only speculative, it may have adorned the bathing complex not far from its findspot.

Examination of these five Roman heads from the Agora sheds light on activities in Athens in the Roman and Byzantine periods. By focusing on these few components of the sculptural assemblages that once filled the public space of Athens, we gain a richer appreciation of the role that portraits played in the ancient city. Whether demonstrating the continued vitality of the Panhellenion in the early 3rd century A.D., or an ongoing interest in the display of Roman imperial propaganda in Athens in the Late Roman period, or the zealotry of Byzantine Christians destroying pagan portraits, these finds show that even after 75 years of excavations in the Athenian Agora, much still remains to discover to improve modern understanding of Athens's past.

Fig. 60
An emperor with a crouching barbarian at his feet,
first quarter of the 2nd century A.D. (S 2518).

The Wine Jars Workroom:
Stamps to Sherds

by Mark L. Lawall

The offices of the Agora excavations on the second floor of the Stoa of Attalos include an archives room, an architect's office, a small library, a conservation laboratory, and an area for photography. Until very recently, however, there was also an office dedicated solely to the study of transport amphoras. These plain clay jars used for shipping and storing wine, oil, and other foodstuffs are frequently found at archaeological sites, but the excavation research facilities rarely include an office dedicated to their study.

This anomalous situation was partly testament to the influence of Virginia Grace (Fig. 61), who began working at the Agora in 1932 and continued, with few interruptions, until her death in 1994. Although Grace was not the first to recognize the importance of studying transport amphoras (and, in particular, the stamps often found impressed on their handles), she did largely define the methods and priorities of the modern discipline. The idea of an office dedicated to one class of artifact was a holdover from the earlier days of the old excavation house compound, where Grace and her assistants used a large part of the second floor, including a Rhodian room and a Knidian room, named after particular types of amphora (Fig. 62). Thus the Wine Jars room carried on a tradition first established in the 1930s and otherwise largely lost when the project moved into the new accommodations of the Stoa of Attalos.

For about a decade after Grace's death, her office in the Stoa of Attalos continued to hold her files and papers, and her assistant Maria Savvatianou-Petropoulakou continued to update the files and host the many visiting researchers who had come to benefit from Grace's decades of gathering data on amphoras and their stamps. In 2001–2002, however, more space was needed for other activities in the Stoa, especially the Agora's massive effort to digitize the excavation records. Grace's files moved to the

Archives of the American School of Classical Studies.

This changing role of the Wine Jars office is a transitional marker in the history of the discipline. Recent work, while depending very much on the work of Grace and her colleagues, has moved in two rather different directions: (1) focusing on the Agora amphoras as groups of potsherds from specific contexts that contribute to a developing picture of Athenian commerce rather than focusing on classes of amphora (e.g., those from Rhodes, Thasos, etc.), and (2) focusing on the amphoras more as pots and less as carriers of inscriptions. Neither of these

Fig. 61
Virginia Grace in 1976. She first joined the Agora staff in 1932 while working toward the completion of her Ph.D. at Bryn Mawr College. Her life's work was the study of transport amphoras. Photograph by Eugene Vanderpool Jr.

Fig. 62

Work in the «Rhodian amphora room» in the Old Excavation House, July 1950. Ch. Andreades and M. Savvatianou-Petropoulakou (seated), Ch. Papadopoulou-Kanellopoulou and A. Dimoulinis (standing). The dedication of so much space to the study of one class of artifact was an unusual feature of the Agora excavations.

directions was entirely ignored by Grace, whose work and that of her colleagues is reviewed in the first part of this chapter. Instead, the extent to which these are new directions depends more on the priorities of current research, as discussed in the conclusion of the first section. The second part of this chapter illustrates these changing priorities through consideration of the foundation fills for the enigmatic Underground Chamber on the west side of the Panathenaic Way.

Amphora Studies at the Agora

Fig. 63
Maria Savvatianou-Petropoulakou sorting amphora stamps in the National Museum in Athens, 1953.

Over her six-decade career of gathering data related to transport amphoras and their stamps, Virginia Grace accumulated and rigorously organized documentation of hundreds of thousands of examples. With such resources, she and her colleagues were able to restore poorly preserved stamps and to arrange stamps from the various classes (Thasian, Rhodian, Koan, Knidian, etc.) in appropriate relative and absolute chronological order. Countless visiting scholars not only contributed new examples to the files but also used the information contained in the files to publish their own material. The evidence that Grace was able to pull from the amphora stamps came to influence numerous aspects of Classical and Hellenistic archaeological chronologies in the Mediterranean. Today, the chronology of nearly every site of these periods (5th–2nd centuries B.C.) in the eastern Mediterranean depends at least in part on Grace's work.

Over the course of the first six decades of excavation at the Athenian Agora many other scholars became involved in amphora research. Among early collaborators were Maria Savvatianou-Petropoulakou and Andreas Dimoulinis, both of whom continued to assist Grace until 1994 and continued to update her files for some time thereafter. Charikleia Papadopoulos-Kanellopoulou and Christos Andreades also assisted Grace's research in the early postwar years. Petropoulakou was the coauthor on the publication of the Delos amphora stamps in 1970. She also made numerous research trips to gather photographs and other documentation from a wide range of sites, including Rhodes and Alexandria (Fig. 63). Dimoulinis provided countless visiting scholars with restorations of stamp readings, particularly those of Rhodian stamps, and he provided significant assistance to Grace's research (Fig. 64). Papadopoulos-Kanellopoulou, who helped organize the National Museum's collection of amphora stamps between 1949 and 1952, became an important scholar of Attic black-figure vases, with two major monographs appearing in the past decade.

One of the earliest projects to branch off from Grace's studies in the early 1950s was Elizabeth Lyding Will's study of Italian stamped amphoras in the eastern Mediterranean, with a particular focus on Athens, Delos, and Alexandria. The rapidly expanding field of Roman amphora studies drew her attention to other sites, such as Cosa, and regions, including India, so that what began at the Agora as a neatly defined topic became increasingly difficult to complete.

In the early 1970s Carolyn Koehler embarked on the study of Corinthian amphoras, and in 1978 she completed her catalogue of examples especially from Athens and Corinth but including examples from across the Mediterranean. Koehler became increasingly involved in all aspects of Grace's research, with much of her most recent work focusing on the assembly of the corpus of Knidian amphora stamps.

Koehler also worked closely with Philippa Wallace Matheson and Malcolm Wallace. Matheson began assisting Grace in Athens and on research trips in 1961. In 1986 Koehler and Matheson began the digitization of Grace's research files. Matheson established and maintains the AMPHORAS project Web site.

Malcolm Wallace followed up Grace's interest in standard amphora capacities. Grace and others believed that the stamps certified the standard, perhaps minimum acceptable, capacity of the jar in question. Wallace, along with Koehler, Matheson, and Barbara Johnson, developed more precise and repeatable methods of capacity measurement. They demonstrated the potential degree of precision in amphora capacities and explored the interaction between amphora capacities and historical circumstances.

Amphora capacities played a significant role, too, in Mabel Lang's work on commercial graffiti and

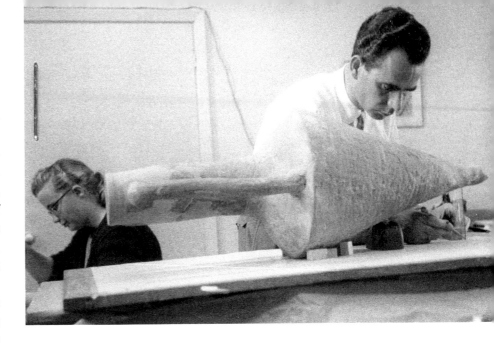

Fig. 64
Andreas Dimoulinis drawing
a Chian amphora, with
Philippa Wallace Matheson
in the background, 1961.
Philippa Matheson and
Carolyn Koehler continue
Virginia Grace's work today
through the AMPHORAS
project.

dipinti at the Agora. Lang, Grace, and later Wallace all argued that the Athenian decree requiring allies to use Athenian coinage, weights, and measures should have had a visible impact on amphora standards among Athens's allies. This idea remains one of great interest to historians of the Peloponnesian War.

Grace's influence also extended to Barbara Clinkenbeard's research on the amphoras of Lesbos, Sally Roberts's study of the amphoras in the Stoa Gutter Well, and Susan Rotroff's studies of Hellenistic pottery in general.

After Grace's death in 1994, work on amphoras at the Agora continued to develop. Current research differs from that of Grace and her colleagues in three main aspects. First, the current work places far more emphasis on assemblages of amphoras and amphora fragments, comparing the makeup of contemporary assemblages and noting changes in assemblages through time. Counting rims, toes, and handles from each dated deposit can reveal trends in imports to Athens as well as changing practices among producers/exporters. Through an Athenian lens, the local economies of Chios, Mende, Lesbos, and other sources of the amphoras found in the Agora can be studied. Today's researchers thus go beyond the older aim of compiling a corpus of amphoras found in 5th-century Athens to build and interpret a group of «sample assemblages» from which to explore economic trends.

A second difference between past and present is the greater emphasis now on the uninventoried context pottery. There are many pieces illustrating amphora shape development and fabric variation still stored in the boxes and tins in the basement of the Stoa of Attalos. Furthermore, despite episodes of selective discard of some context pottery, statistically significant patterns do remain in the compositions of different deposits.

Finally, the current work places much more emphasis on the variation in form and appearance of fabric as exhibited in smaller, but still diagnostic, fragments than in the past. Despite these differences, the work being carried out today builds on the innovative techniques of the 1930s pioneers, as the example of the Underground Chamber (deposit N 10:2) demonstrates.

Amphoras and the Underground Chamber

On a detailed plan of the Agora in the mid-2nd century A.D., a series of monument bases appears between the Panathenaic Way and the Odeion of Agrippa. One of these was excavated in 1935 and restudied starting in 1967 by John Camp (Fig. 65). It has a solidly built stone floor and well-cut, carefully joined stone walls. Blocks, likely meant to support a floor or roof, project into the room from the west wall. Five stele bases line the east side facing the Panathenaic Way and these seem to have been put in place at different times, to judge from the stratigraphic layers underlying some of them but not others. Camp observed that this monument base, like its two neighbors, may have been aligned along an earlier orientation of the Panathenaic Way, and he wondered if it might have been a tomb, cenotaph, or heroon. No date has ever been offered for

this structure, and without that information it is difficult to refine the identification or interpretation of the structure.

Arriving at a date for the building, however, is not difficult. The foundation fills were excavated in 1935 and later assigned a deposit designation «N 10:2». There were no coins and very little in the way of fine pottery, so the date of the deposit depends on the amphoras (Figs. 66–68). Grace's report concludes:

«This deposit is contemporary with [Homer] Thompson's [Hesperia 1934] Group B, i.e., not later than 250 and probably nearer 300. (The stamped jars belonged to the earliest part of the Group B deposit.) The association is based on the occurrences in both deposits of largely preserved jars bearing rose stamps of the maker Zeno.»

Grace's revised Hellenistic chronology, published in 1974, placed group B (and hence deposit N 10:2) as closing around 240 B.C., so the Underground Chamber should have been constructed about the same time.

Reconsideration of the contents of N 10:2 in light of subsequent revisions to the Rhodian amphora chronology further refines the likely date of its filling and hence the date of the Underground Chamber. A wider view of the contents of the deposit expands our understanding of Athenian imports in the Hellenistic period.

The most readily datable pieces in the deposit are the Rhodian stamped amphoras (Fig. 66). The two latest datable stamps are of the annual magistrates Agloukritos, now dated by Gérald Finkielsztejn around 216 B.C., and Sochares, dated near 218 B.C. A widely bulging neck fragment from Knidos

Fig. 66
Selected Rhodian am-
phora fragments from
N 10:2. From left to
right: SS 3784 and 3711
stamped with the eponym
Sochares; SS 3793 with
the eponym Kallikratidas
(I); and SS 3804 with
the eponym Kallikrates
(I).

⇨ Fig. 67
Other amphoras from
N 10:2. Representatives
of the Nikandros group
(SS 3807) and Parmenis-
kos group (SS 3791).

is typical of the middle to late 3rd century B.C.,
and the same general range of dates is appropriate
for the two rim fragments from Erythrai. Likewise,
the Nikandros group fragments have parallels in
late 3rd-century strata at Ephesos, their likely place
of production. The Parmeniskos group stamp of
Sokrates is not closely datable, but most of these
stamps appear around the middle of the 3rd century
B.C. (Fig. 67).

A number of points stand out about this deposit
in terms of trends in imports of amphoras to Athens
throughout the Hellenistic period. Most important,
this is one of a few late 3rd-century B.C. deposits
that finally start to show, in Athens, the typically
Hellenistic dominance of Rhodian imports. Although there are earlier Rhodian amphora stamps
found in Athens, the Rhodian presence for much
of the 3rd century is negligible compared with finds

Fig. 68
Italian amphoras from
N 10:2. The larger
fragment is P 35285;
the smaller is P 35284.

of other types. This scarcity of Rhodian amphoras in Athens is especially striking when compared with sites along the southwestern coast of Turkey.

Similarly, Corinthian and western Mediterranean amphoras in the N 10:2 assemblage foreshadow a fairly gradual rise in imports from the West through the 2nd century. N 10:2 is not the earliest deposit to show such imports, but it is the first to include them on any noticeable level after the late 5th century B.C. (Fig. 68).

The rare presence of Pontic amphoras — fragments of only two or three amphoras from Sinope — is typical of the 3rd-century deposits in Athens. Despite the well-known Athenian interest in Black Sea grain, Pontic amphoras are nearly absent from Agora deposits before the 3rd century B.C., and even during the 3rd century they are never common.

The contents of N 10:2 date the Underground Chamber to the last decade or so of the 3rd century B.C., and they highlight important trends in the history of amphora imports to Athens. The date of the structure also allows its reconsideration in terms of the historical or commemorative topography of the Agora.

First, the empty space on the plan for the 2nd-century B.C. Agora should be filled in with this and likely a few other monuments along the Panathenaic Way. If this was an honorific monument of some sort, we should be looking for candidates in the last decade or so of the 3rd century. Gerald Lalonde draws attention to Eurykleides of Kephisia's activities in cultic renewal after ca. 229 B.C., and it may be possible to link the N 10:2 monument with this movement. And yet, whereas Grace's Rhodian chronology would have placed the closing date in the 220s, Finkielsztejn's lower chronology places the closing in the 210s, and even this slightly later date raises the possibility that the monument was not solely relevant to Athens. Christian Habicht has observed the increasingly frequent commemoration of Athenian-Pergamene friendship at the end of the 3rd century. David Scahill has pointed out that the later donor's monument in front of the Stoa of Attalos is due west of the N 10:2 structure. Kevin Daly notes that a rare honorific decree for a Rhodian, datable to ca. 200 B.C., may be related to the return of the Tyrannicides statue group to Athens and that this statue group was likely placed near N 10:2. A further indication of the nature of the N 10:2 monument may be provided by the inscription published by Susan Rotroff in 1978. That text refers to furniture, linens, and silver vessels having been deposited in the shrine of a hero. The N 10:2 monument is not the recipient monument in question, but such a chamber would be quite suitable as a strongbox for dedications.

Conclusion

Deposit N 10:2 and the Underground Chamber provide a tangible link between the traditions of past scholarship at the Athenian Agora, new interests building on that past, and resulting new evidence that may lead to even more exciting results in the not too distant future. Virginia Grace was able to link the finds from N 10:2 into the chronological scheme that Homer Thompson published for Hellenistic pottery in 1934. Further revisions and refinements to this chronology now allow us to date N 10:2 near the very end of the 3rd century B.C.

We can use N 10:2 as an example to characterize late 3rd-century B.C. Athenian amphora imports in comparison to other sites around the Aegean. This long-ago excavated deposit is now contributing to answering new questions about Athenian and Aegean trading patterns. At the same time, the newly refined dating of the deposit may make it possible to fill in a significant gap in our understanding of the cultural topography of the city center of ancient Athens.

The Persian Destruction Deposits and the Development of Pottery Research at the Agora Excavations

by Kathleen M. Lynch

Think about your week's garbage: what will an archaeologist of the future deduce about your dining habits, entertainment preferences, or even beauty regimen? Ancient pottery permits a similar view into the ordinary lives of Greeks. Ceramics are the plastics of antiquity. Baked clay is just as versatile and durable as plastic is today and from it potters fashioned a great variety of everyday and special-use objects. Just as the shapes of plastic soda bottles have changed over time (themselves an innovation after many years of glass bottles and then aluminum cans), so too do ceramics change over time. Thus, one of the primary archaeological uses of pottery is to indicate the date of an excavation layer based on knowledge of the development of pottery shapes and styles. But this is not the only contribution pottery makes to archaeological study.

At the Agora excavations we are fortunate to have one particularly rich horizon of pottery that has been associated with the most important historical event in the life of Athens's young democracy: the Persian invasion and destruction of Athens. Scholars first studied the pottery from the clean-up following the destruction in 480/79 B.C. to establish typologies and chronologies, that is, to organize them by shape and offer dates for their production; now we are asking questions about their original context and cultural meaning. Questions of use, audience, identity, function, and other topics would not be possible for pottery from the Agora without these fundamental typological and chronological studies. Scholarship by Agora excavation researchers has both responded to and directed many dimensions of ceramic studies throughout the Mediterranean.

Discovery and Identification

In the earliest years of archaeological exploration in the Athenian Agora, excavators recognized the historical and cultural value of the debris attributed to the clean-up following the Persian destruction of Athens. In the second year of excavations, 25-year-old Eugene Vanderpool began excavating what would be called the Rectangular Rock-Cut Shaft (G 6:3) (Fig. 69). In his notebook, Vanderpool remarked, «The fill in the shaft appears to be a gradual accumulation over a period of some 75 years – from the middle of the sixth century to B.C. 480». He soon published a selection of the more than 500 inventoried pieces of black-figure, red-figure, black-glaze, and household-ware pottery, developing the idea that the upper most level of the deposit was associated with the cleanup of debris following the Persian destruction. German excavators had identified a Persian destruction clean-up layer from the Acropolis, and although the fill there contained spectacular Archaic sculptures, the pottery from this fill was highly fragmentary and seemed to be mixed with later Classical pottery. Thus, the Persian destruction debris from the Agora excavations provided a welcome complement to and check on the Acropolis debris layers.

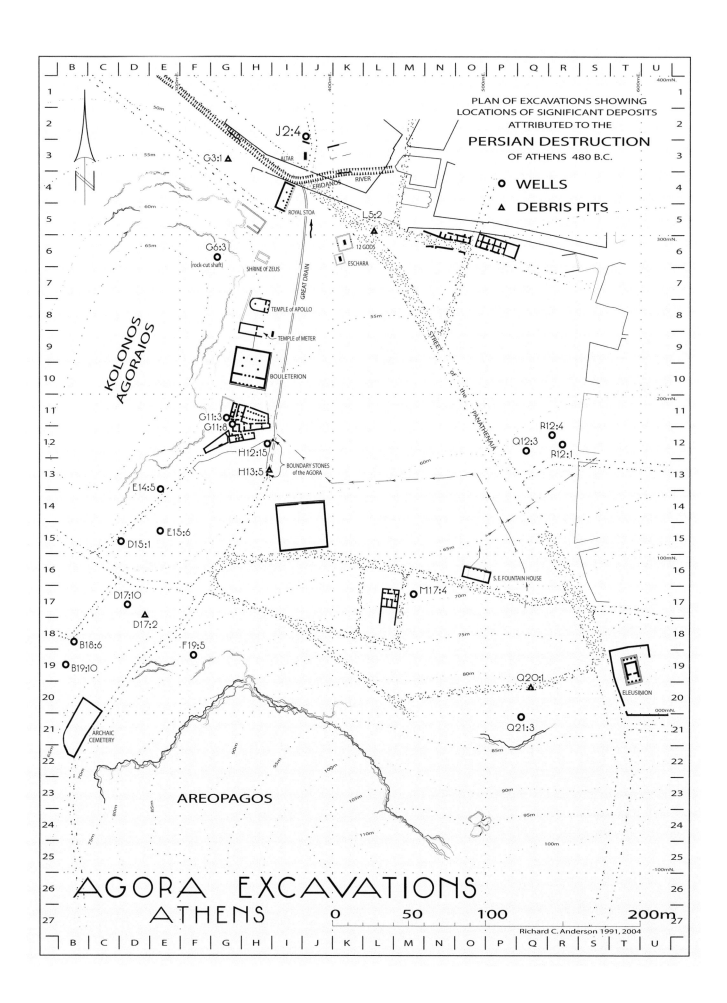

PLAN OF EXCAVATIONS SHOWING
LOCATIONS OF SIGNIFICANT DEPOSITS
ATTRIBUTED TO THE
PERSIAN DESTRUCTION
OF ATHENS 480 B.C.

○ WELLS

▲ DEBRIS PITS

J2:4

G3:1 ▲

ALTAR

ERIDANOS RIVER

ROYAL STOA

L5:2 ▲

G6:3
(rock-cut shaft)

12 GODS

SHRINE of ZEUS

ESCHARA

GREAT DRAIN

TEMPLE of APOLLO

TEMPLE of METER

KOLONOS AGORAIOS

BOULETERION

G11:3
G11:8

H12:15

H13:5 ▲

BOUNDARY STONES
of the AGORA

E14:5

STREET of the PANATHENAIA

R12:4
Q12:3
R12:1

E15:6

D15:1

D17:10

D17:2

S.E. FOUNTAIN HOUSE

M17:4

B18:6

F19:5

Q20:1

B19:10

ELEUSINION

ARCHAIC
CEMETERY

Q21:3

AREOPAGOS

AGORA EXCAVATIONS
ATHENS

0   50   100   200m

Richard C. Anderson 1991, 2004

Vanderpool associated the fill in his Rectangular Rock-Cut Shaft not only with a historical event but also with known historical figures. Ostraka of Hippokrates, Megakles, Aristeides, and Themistokles were found in the shaft, which represented the first group of men for whom literary sources provided ostracism dates. Vanderpool assumed that the ostraka originated from the years in which those candidates were ostracized and used the difference in date to argue for a slow fill of the shaft. His instinct was correct, but now we allow that a man could receive votes in years preceding the year of his actual ostracism. As we will see, fifty years after its discovery, a reinterpretation of the Rectangular Rock-Cut Shaft's ostraka dates would add fuel to a controversial movement to downdate Greek material culture.

⇦ Fig. 69 Plan showing location of archaeological deposits known to date from the clean-up after the destruction of Athens at the hands of the Persians in 480/79 B.C.

Vanderpool and others were eager to associate the archaeological record with historical events. The Agora excavations have been criticized for an over reliance on historical texts, but the Persian destruction deposits demonstrate that the rich historical record available to Agora researchers permits a degree of chronological sensitivity that is rare for most sites. In addition, the historical background truly allows the archaeological record to come alive, not just with generic inhabitants but with known individuals.

Subsequent discoveries of wells and pits filled with pottery similar in character to Vanderpool's Rectangular Rock-Cut Shaft helped to reinforce his identification of the fill as debris generated from the cleanup following the Persian destruction. Other deposits of debris included two wells associated with building F, the predecessor of the Tholos, the circular meetinghouse of the Athenian *prytany* (G 11:3 and G 11:8); and wells associated with private houses. Renovation of the Stoa of Attalos in 1954 revealed a well that was filled with as much pottery as the Rectangular Rock-Cut Shaft, providing

Fig. 70
Stoa of Attalos Gutter Well pottery in mending room of the Old Excavation House. This large quantity of material came from just one deposit, Q 12:3.

Fig. 71
Pottery storage at the Old Excavation House, with Lucy Talcott at her desk. With her colleague Brian Sparkes, Talcott made a lasting contribution to scholarship in her publication of the undecorated pottery of the Archaic and Classical periods.

Fig. 72
Group of «lekythoi» (the «lekythos» is a type of narrow vase for storing oil) from the well beneath the Stoa of Attalos (Q 12:3). It has been argued that this deposit reflects debris from a shop selling pottery.

further evidence for the homogeneity of the horizon of debris deposits (Q 12:3).

Meanwhile, the vast and growing quantity of pottery associated with the Persian destruction of Athens provided a firm basis for the creation of chronological and typological studies (Fig. 70). At the time of the Persian invasion, Athens was exporting fine pottery throughout the Mediterranean and beyond. Although the Persian destruction deposits are not the only closed deposits from the Agora excavations, the abundance of pottery from them permitted Lucy Talcott and Brian Sparkes to offer more detailed refinement of Late Archaic pottery typologies and chronologies than for other periods covered by their volume, *The Black and Plain Pottery of the 6th, 5th, and 4th Centuries B.C.* (Fig. 71). As a result, excavators digging in all corners of the ancient world rejoice when they find Archaic and Classical Attic pottery, which in turn can help them date their finds of regionally produced pottery.

The figured wares in the Persian destruction deposits permitted refinement of vase painting stylistic chronologies, but they also advanced our understanding of pottery-producing workshops. Excavators suggested that two of the Persian destruction deposits represent the debris from pottery shops, Vanderpool's Rectangular Rock-Cut Shaft and what we call the Stoa Gutter Well, the deposit from under the Stoa of Attalos. They were not pottery factories but rather salesrooms predominantly for black-figure wares with only a few red-figure vessels present (Fig. 72). A study of the «hands» of the vase painters and potters present in these deposits showed that individual vase painters worked in collaboration with one or more potters, and the shops handled pottery from a limited range of producers. Traditional vase painting study combined with attention to archaeological context revealed new information about pottery production and sales in Athens.

Challenges to Dating

In the late 1980s and early 1990s, Michael Vickers, David Francis, and David Gill proposed a dramatic redating of many works of Greek sculpture and vase painting, concluding that several Persian destruction deposits contained material produced in the decades after the Persian wars, meaning that pottery in them should be dated 25 years later to ca. 475–450, not 500–479 B.C. as originally proposed. Their conclusions were based on a reconsideration of the ostracism dates of the Rectangular Rock-Cut Shaft ostraka, and the proposal that the Persians built the Rock-Cut Shaft, not the Greeks. A masterful 1993 study by T. Leslie Shear Jr., of 21 closed Persian destruction deposits, however, showed that these deposits are truly uniform in the character and the date range of their contents, and that the overwhelming evidence indicates that the majority of the deposits were closed ca. 479 B.C., following a catastrophic event.

The challenge to the original dating had raised awareness of some critical chronological issues. First, scholars date the red-figure pottery in most of the deposits stylistically to ca. 500 B.C., whereas they date much of the black-figure to ca. 480 B.C. This discrepancy deserves more attention, and the Persian destruction deposits may hold some answers.

Second, Shear's study identified several deposits that were not closed immediately after the wars. In these exceptions, the majority of the pottery is dated before 480 B.C., but the deposits contained some objects dating to 470 B.C. and occasionally later. These delayed deposits give us a realistic view of Athenians returning to their devastated city and cleaning up at varying paces. Surely we will see piles of debris in the Gulf Coast area for many years after Hurricane Katrina.

Shear also drew attention to the fact that many of the deposits contained material that originated in private Athenian houses. Thus, even in mounting a defense of the identification and dating of the Persian destruction deposits, Shear considered both the original context of use for the material and the function of the wells. His approach took history as its background but moved beyond a pedantic dating argument and located the ancient people and households present in the ordinary aspects of the archaeological record.

New Trends in Pottery Research

A tide has recently turned in pottery research toward the study of objects in their historical, cultural, or functional context. Dating of pottery and connoisseurship, in the case of figured wares, were important first steps, but they are no longer the only steps in ceramic studies. New questions focus on the nature of the deposits: that is, the processes that formed them and the activities they represent. Susan Rotroff and John Oakley's 1992 study of a later 5th-century B.C. deposit — although not a Persian destruction deposit — from the west side of the Agora is a key example of this mode of inquiry. The authors provide the requisite typological and chronological study of the pottery but situate the deposit historically and in the social context of public dining.

Questions of context and meaning extend beyond fine wares. Even transport amphoras from the Persian destruction deposits, when examined as household or commercial equipment, can inform questions of economy and cultural consumption of commodities. Mark Lawall, in particular, has examined the graffiti that many of the jars bear to understand how they functioned in the house. Barbara Tsakirgis, in her study of private housing in the area of the Agora, considers the entire household assemblage — that is, the coarse, fine, and figured pottery and their associated artifacts — as a reflection of cultural activities. Some of this work is reflected in Chapter 3.

The study of vase painting has only recently embraced the importance of context to the interpretation of images. Now that we are correlating patterns of images with find locations, we recognize that who viewed a vase's image and in what context they viewed it can reveal culturally significant meanings. For example, a study of one of the Persian destruction deposits, well J 2:4, examines all the pottery in the household and considers both the overall meaning of the figured pottery's imagery and the relationship of the figured pottery to the plain and coarse pottery for this one household (Figs. 73 and 74). Importantly, the Persian destruction deposits do not contain a cross-section of all vase painting images produced at the time; instead, the deposits contain a consistent subset of themes, which include, for example, far more «genre» scenes (showing everyday life) than mythological scenes. The contextual approach allows us to understand choices real Athenians made and, in turn, more accurately reflects their cultural perspectives.

How will the study of the Persian destruction deposits evolve in the future? The deposits certainly have potential to answer more questions about everyday activities and entertaining in the household. In addition, it is very likely that Agora excavators will find new Persian destruction deposits. But what could yet another deposit tell us? Excavators kept all the material from the most recently excavated deposit, J 2:4, permitting quantification of its contents. In contrast, earlier excavators frequently discarded the coarse wares or nondiagnostic fine-ware body sherds from deposits. Statistical analysis of another new deposit would help characterize typical household assemblages for the Late Archaic period. Palaeobotanical remains and organic residues from the vessels could not be recovered from deposit J 2:4, but a new deposit might allow archaeological science to inform us more about diet and perhaps even the reason that so many household wells were closed after the withdrawal of the Persians. (It has been speculated that the Persians poisoned the household wells with horse feces. If this is true, palaeobotanical remains could confirm it.)

Fig. 73
Group photo of objects from well J 2:4. This deposit probably represents pottery from a single household.

⇩ Fig. 74
«Kylixes» from well J 2:4. The «kylix» is a type of shallow cup particularly associated with «symposia», or drinking parties.

At the Agora we recognize the importance of traditional, some would say conservative, approaches to identifying type, chronology, and attribution of pottery. We cannot abandon those fundamental assessments, but rather we must use them to answer new questions. There is no escaping the pottery catalogue, but it should be a tool, not an end. There is value in reexamining «old» material, using pottery excavated and even published a generation ago to answer «new» questions that earlier scholars could not fathom. As we continue to develop sophisticated questions about the relationship of the ancient material world to cultural activities, the Persian destruction deposit pottery will provide future generations of scholars with fertile and abundant ground for questions.

Ostraka from the Athenian Agora

by James P. Sickinger

Few finds from the Agora excavations have attracted as much attention as the *ostraka* (pottery sherds used in the ancient Athenian practice of ostracism) uncovered in and around the ancient marketplace. Even fewer objects have had as direct an impact on our knowledge of the inner workings of Athenian democracy. When excavations in the Agora began in 1931 no more than 50 *ostraka* were known, and scholars of ancient history relied primarily on literary sources for their understanding of ostracism's background and operation. Within a decade the Agora had yielded more than 500 *ostraka*, and today that total stands at more than 1,500. These finds, together with *ostraka* found in other parts of Athens, illustrate many of the features of ostracism as that practice is known from literary tradition. But they also highlight aspects of ostracism and Athenian politics not hinted at by ancient texts, and thus have substantially enhanced modern understanding of this peculiar institution.

Ostracism was, at least on paper, a simple practice. Each year, the Athenians decided if they wanted to hold a vote of ostracism, an *ostrakaphoria*, which would result in the exile of one citizen. If they decided to hold such a vote, they gathered again two months later in the Agora, each voter bringing with him a potsherd (*ostrakon*) on which he had incised the name of a citizen he wanted sent into exile. A quorum of 6,000 votes was required for a vote to be considered valid, and, if a quorum was reached, the candidate with the most votes had to leave Athens for 10 years, after which he could return to the city with his property and rights intact.

The lawgiver Kleisthenes was credited with creating ostracism in 508/7 B.C. as a tool against potential tyrants, but the first vote was not held until 20 years later, in 487 B.C. Votes conducted in years that followed and throughout the 5th century B.C. allowed the Athenian people to exile politicians who were thought to pose a threat to civic order or who had simply fallen out of favor. The last ostracism was held between 417 and 415 B.C. (the exact year is unknown). At that time, Nikias and Alkibiades, two of the leading statesmen of the time, joined forces and engineered the exile of the less prominent politician Hyperbolos. The Athenians were so disgusted at this abuse of ostracism and its use against a figure so undeserving of exile that, although they kept the law on ostracism on the books, they never resorted to it again.

Potsherds as Ballots

The durability of the pottery sherds used as ballots means that they survive in large numbers, and more than 11,000 have been found in Athens — about 1,500 in the Agora and its environs and nearly 10,000 more in the Kerameikos, northwest of the Agora. These *ostraka* come in all shapes and sizes and from all sorts of vessels, but they are usually small enough to fit in the palm of one's hand.

Texts are normally scratched into one surface of a sherd (a few painted examples are known), and they normally include a candidate's name followed by either his patronymic (his father's name) or, less commonly, his demotic (the deme or village from which his family came); a small number of *ostraka* include both. The oldest *ostraka* date from the first ostracism of 487 B.C., when Hipparchos son of Charmos, a relation of the exiled tyrant Peisistratos, was banished, and most of those found in and around the Agora belong to the 480s B.C., when votes of ostracism were conducted regularly. The large number from this decade is almost a certainly a result of the use of *ostraka* as fill in the cleaning and building activities that took place upon the return of the Athenians to their city after its sack by the Persians in 480 and 479 B.C. But the Agora excavations have also uncovered *ostraka* from other *ostrakaphoriai* of the 5th century B.C., and the full history of the institution is represented by the ballots discarded after they had been counted.

Ostraka started to appear in large numbers almost as soon as excavations began in the Agora, and the first finds brought to life features of ostracism known from, or mentioned in, literary sources. The

dates of excavated *ostraka* fell within the period in which the practice was said to have been in use, and their discovery in and around the Agora itself confirmed ancient reports that *ostrakaphoriai* were held in the marketplace. The names on many sherds also affirmed traditions that many of the leading statesmen of the 5th century — Aristeides, Kimon, Themistokles, Perikles, and others — were candidates for ostracism (Fig. 75). Other, less well-known candidates also appeared on some *ostraka* and proved especially welcome discoveries. One such candidate was Kallias son of Didymias. A speech attributed to the orator Andokides states that the Athenians had ostracized Kallias ([And.] 4.32), but historians questioned that speech's reliability and the historicity of Kallias's exile because of his relative obscurity. Discovery of *ostraka* with his name did not prove the authenticity of Andokides' report, but it did lend the tradition of Kallias's ostracism some support by showing that some ancient Athenians considered him a potential candidate.

As excavations continued and the number of *ostraka* grew, it also became clear that these incised sherds could also shed light on the practice of ostracism, and on other areas of Athenian society, in new

Fig. 75
Many of the leading statesmen of the 5th century B.C. may have been candidates for ostracism, as shown by these four «ostraka». From left to right, and top to bottom: «ostrakon» of Aristeides (P 9973), «ostrakon» of Kimon (P 18555), «ostrakon» of Perikles (P 16755), and «ostrakon» of Themistokles (P 9950).

and unexpected ways. Consider, for example, the writing on these sherds. Because most *ostraka* appear to have been written by individual Athenians, their texts offer invaluable and often unparalleled information about spelling, pronunciation, and the general writing habits of Athenian citizens. The earliest *ostraka* are written in the old Attic alphabet, which lacks the letters *eta* and *omega* and has different characters for *gamma and lambda* than the Ionic alphabet, which was officially adopted at Athens only at the end of the 5th century B.C. Ionic letter forms are rare in the earliest *ostraka* but grow more common as the century advances, a sign that private use of Ionic forms by citizens in daily life preceded their official adoption. The spelling of names on different *ostraka* also fluctuates widely. Candidates like Hipparchos, Hippokrates, and Xanthippos have their names spelled with either one pi or two, while *ostraka* for Kallias, Kallixenos, and Eratyllos sometime have a single *lambda*, sometimes two. Unusual spellings also provide clues to pronunciation, as in the case of *ostraka* for Themistokles. In literary texts his name is invariably spelled with a *tau* in the third syllable – Themistokles. But in the vast majority of the Agora *ostraka* that medial *tau* is replaced with a *theta* – Themisthokles. In this case the *ostraka* probably illustrate not a misspelling but the actual pronunciation of Themistokles' name in his own time.

Some voters also appended comments to their ballots along with the names of candidates and in this way provided an indication of the reasons behind their votes. The author of one *ostrakon* for Xanthippos discovered in the first decade of the Agora excavations explained his vote as follows: «This *ostrakon* says that Xanthippos, the son of

Fig. 76
An «ostrakon» of Xanthippos (P 16873), labeling him «the most accursed of the prytaneis». This is an example of the way in which some voters appended comments to their ballots along with the names of candidates and in this way provided an indication of the reasons behind their vote.

Ariphron, the most accursed of the prytaneis, does wrong most of all» (Fig. 76). The precise nature of Xanthippos's wrongdoing is not specified, but it was evidently sufficient to rouse this voter's ire. Other *ostraka* are briefer but no less pointed; one *ostrakon* appends to the name of its intended victim the word *itō* («let him go!»), while another labels its candidate *prodotês*, a traitor. Commentary of this sort is even more common on *ostraka* from the Kerameikos, where voters remark on everything from the alleged pro-Persian leanings of candidates to their sexual proclivities. Isolated comments of this nature may be the product of personal grudges or a voter's deep personal dislike for a particular candidate, and it would be a mistake to see in them sentiments widely shared by the Athenian electorate. At the same time, these remarks offer glimpses into the thinking of individual voters in ways that literary sources fail to do.

«Ostraka» and Athenian Politics

The extant *ostraka* also supply new information on the politics of 5th-century Athens, from the dates of specific ostracisms to the pool of potential candidates in a given year. Several ancient sources, for example, mention that Alkibiades the Elder, grandfather of the famous Alkibiades who served as general in the Peloponnesian War, was a victim of ostracism. They do not, however, give the year or period in which he was banished. Before excavations in the Agora began, the elder Alkibiades' exile had been put in 485 B.C., a year in which, according to Aristotle, an unnamed «friend of the tyrants» was ostracized. But when sherds with this Alkibiades' name were discovered, they were found not alongside *ostraka* of candidates of the 480s but in contexts dating from the third quarter of the 5th century (ca. 475–450 B.C.). Some of these *ostraka* even came from *kylikes* (a type of cup) that first came into use in the 460s. As a result, the ostracism and career of the elder Alkibiades had to be downdated from the 480s to the late 460s B.C., and his name could be eliminated from consideration as the unknown victim of the *ostrakaphoria* of 485 B.C.

The number of candidates at any given *ostrakophoria* is also now known to have been much larger than ever anticipated. Literary sources tend to portray votes as referenda on a single candidate or as contests pitting two political rivals and their policies against one another. The discovery of *ostraka* with the names of prominent Athenians confirms their candidacies, but other *ostraka* show that a vote of ostracism also produced ballots against a much wider range of candidates, including persons about whom little or absolutely nothing else is known. Some individuals are named on a small number or even a single sherd, and the votes against them may be isolated or exceptional cases, the product not of political disagreement but purely personal enmity. But a few obscure individuals are represented on a fairly large number of *ostraka*, and the numbers against them suggest that we are dealing with persons who were real candidates and potential victims.

Two such men are Hippokrates son of Alkmeonides and Kallixenos son of Aristonymos. Neither man is mentioned in any literary source, but the names of their fathers link both to the Alkmeonid clan, a prominent Athenian family whose more famous members included the statesmen Kleisthenes and Perikles. *ostraka* for Hippokrates and Kallixenos have been found alongside ones for Hipparchos, Themistokles, Xanthippos, and Aristeides, all of whom were candidates for ostracism in the 480s, when Hippokrates and Kallixenos must also have been candidates. The number of sherds with their names, however, is remarkable given their anonymity: Hippokrates is named on more than 100 Agora *ostraka*, and Kallixenos on almost 300 (Fig. 77). This total is second only to the number for Themistokles. We do not know if either man was ever ostracized, but the number of ballots against them suggests that many Athenians considered them viable candidates, despite the absence of any mention of them in literary texts. The *ostraka* with their names and those of other unknowns is a salutary reminder of the incomplete state of our knowledge of Athenian politics even in the well-documented 5th century B.C.

Fig. 77
The relatively unknown statesmen Hippokrates and Kallixenos were frequent candidates for ostracism in the 480s B.C. Hippokrates is named on more than 100 Agora «ostraka», and Kallixenos on almost 300. The four «ostraka» shown here are examples. From left to right, and top to bottom: «ostrakon» of Hippokrates (P 15593), «ostrakon» of Hippokrates (P 6036), «ostrakon» of Kallixenos (P 5315), and «ostrakon» of Kallixenos (P 32308).

Recent Discoveries at K 2:7

The Agora *ostraka* found in the first 50 years of excavation were published in exemplary fashion by Mabel Lang in 1990, in volume XXV of *The Athenian Agora* series. But research on ostracism and the Agora *ostraka* progresses, as new finds and new publications refine the picture that began to emerge in the early years of the Agora excavations. The most significant development of recent years has been the publication of more detailed information about the *ostraka* from the Kerameikos. Excavations there in the 1960s unearthed a massive deposit of more than 8,000 *ostraka*. Initially assigned a date in the mid-480s, the majority of those *ostraka* now seem to belong to the late 470s, and perhaps to a single ostracism conducted in the year 471 B.C. These finds enormously increase the available evidence for the study of ostracism and supply a welcome sample against which we can compare the Agora *ostraka*. The two assemblages show many similarities in letter forms, spelling, and features of nomenclature, and features of the Kerameikos *ostraka* reinforce many older conclusions drawn on the basis of the Agora finds alone. The Kerameikos *ostraka* also supply more abundant evidence for practices that are observed only occasionally on the Agora *ostraka*. Commentary and insults appear much more frequently on *ostraka* from the Kerameikos, as do portraits, a phenomenon that appears only once on the *ostraka* from the Agora. Some differences, however, do exist. Some names on the Agora and Kerameikos *ostraka* overlap, but each collection also includes *ostraka* for individuals who are poorly attested or not represented in the other. Those differences should say something about the careers of some Athenians, and further study may shed additional light on the changing politics of the 480s and 470s B.C.

The Agora too has produced new finds in recent years. Most noteworthy is a deposit discovered in the late 1990s behind the Stoa Poikile and just east of the Classical Commercial Building. Given the label K 2:7, this deposit produced more than 150 *ostraka*, from which names can be read or restored on some 125 sherds. Five candidates are represented. Themistokles, architect of Athens's victory over the Persians at Salamis in 480 B.C., is named on more than 65 sherds. Just under 60 carry the name of Xanthippos son of Ariphron, a member of the Alkmeonid family, father of Perikles, and a victim of ostracism in 484 B.C.; according to Aristotle he was the first victim who was not a friend of the tyrants. The name of Aristeides son of Lysimachos, who was ostracized in 482 B.C., is found on a single sherd. The two remaining candidates are Hippokrates son of Alkmeonides, whose name and patronymic can be restored on two *ostraka*, and a certain Kydrokles son of Timokrates from the deme Krioa, whose name and demotic can be restored on a single sherd. Neither of the latter two men is known from literary sources, but both are named on other Agora *ostraka*. The *ostraka* for them in this deposit bring welcome attention to the minor figures, otherwise unknown to us, who often attracted a small number of votes.

Had a deposit with these five names been uncovered 20 years ago, it might have been dated to the 480s with little discussion, since Aristeides, Themistokles, and Xanthippos were all candidates for ostracism in that decade. But the careers of Aristeides and Themistokles also extended into the late 470s, and more than 4,000 *ostraka* for Themistokles, and another 50 for Aristeides, were found in the great Kerameikos deposit that is now dated to the 470s; a pre-480 date for *ostraka* for Aristeides and Themistokles cannot be taken for granted. The career of Xanthippos, however, excludes such a late date for K 2:7. Xanthippos rose to prominence in the 480s and was ostracized in 484 B.C. He returned to Athens on the eve of the Persian invasion of 480 B.C. and served as general in 479 and 478 B.C. But he then disappears from the historical record, and it seems that he became politically inactive or died by the mid-470s. The nearly complete absence of *ostraka* with his name from the Kerameikos supports this inference. Only three sherds with his name were found in the large deposit uncovered in the 1960s, and those sherds were found in different contexts than the vast majority of *ostraka* dating to the late 470s; they may be intrusions or remnants from an earlier period. The relatively large number of Xanthippos *ostraka* in K 2:7 (the largest number for him ever found in a single deposit), on the other hand, point to their origin at a time when Xanthippos was politically active and a leading candidate for ostracism. That period is almost certainly the mid-480s and perhaps 484 B.C. itself, the very year that Xanthippos was ostracized.

A pre-480 date for K 2:7 is consistent with a majority of the Agora *ostraka*, most of which come from ostracisms conducted prior to the Persian Wars. But that is not the only feature they share. The *ostraka* of deposit K 2:7 are incised on sherds from the same variety of pots as older finds, the Attic alphabet still predominates, and similar variations in the spelling of names appear. In addition, *ostraka*

for Themistokles always spell his name with a *theta* in its third syllable, and about half identify him by his demotic — exactly the same percentage shown by older Agora *ostraka* with his name. A few of the *ostraka* from K 2:7 also include text in addition to a candidate's name. One *ostrakon* appears to label its intended victim, whose name is lost, *katapugon*, a catamite or younger homosexual partner. Another adds the message that its recipient should «go» or «get out» of Athens. Overall, the picture of ostracism painted by the *ostraka* of K 2:7 conforms very closely to that suggested by earlier discoveries.

«Ostraka» and Ancient Literacy

These new *ostraka* from the Agora may also be relevant to the topic of ancient literacy. Scholars have traditionally assumed that the institution of ostracism, and its requirement that voters submit

written ballots, presupposed widespread literacy in Athens: voters needed to be able to write to participate. Recent scholarship, however, has challenged assumptions of widespread literacy in the ancient

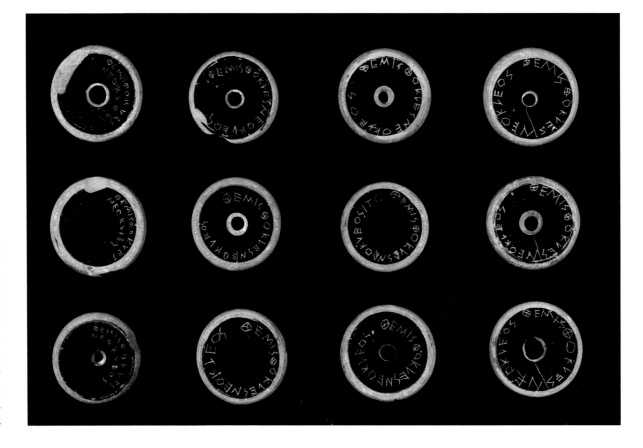

Fig. 78
Twelve «ostraka» of Themistokles, part of a group of 190 bearing the politician's name found in a well on the north slope of the Acropolis. The illustration shows three «ostraka» by each of four different hands. From Ober and Hedrick 1993, p. 104, pl. 15.2–13.

Fig. 79
«Ostraka» of Xanthippos, possibly in the same hand (P 32560, P 32559). The letters are incised deeply and have very similar forms. These may point to the preparation of multiple ballots by single persons.

world, and the relationship between ostracism and literacy requires reconsideration. One deposit of *ostraka* discovered in the 1930s just southeast of the Agora included 190 sherds with the name of Themistokles but written by only 14 different hands (Fig. 78). They seem to have been prepared en masse by opponents of Themistokles for distribution to voters, but they also indicate that citizens did not have to know how to write to participate in a vote of ostracism. A smaller group of seven *ostraka* for Kallixenos likewise show considerable uniformity in the style and arrangement of their writing, and they too appear to be the work of a single individual.

A few *ostraka* from K 2:7 also point to preparation of multiple ballots by single persons. Two ballots for Xanthippos have very deeply incised letters with very similar forms (Fig. 79). Another two *ostraka* for Themistokles come from joining sherds, and their surviving letters also show considerable similarities. Identifying the handwriting of writers based on letters scratched into sherds of pottery is a difficult task, but these finds show that citizens did not have to rely on their own writing skills to participate. Other citizens were ready to supply premade

ostraka, perhaps for both undecided and illiterate voters.

And yet we must be cautious before taking the evidence of these few sherds too far. Most of the 150 sherds of K 2:7 exhibit significant variations in style, spelling, and fabric. Ballots for Themistokles, for example, spell his name sometimes with a single epsilon in the final syllable, sometimes with two; the name of Xanthippos can be spelled with one pi or two. Some *ostraka* are very lightly incised, with text barely penetrating the surface of a sherd, and in some cases writing can be so faint or sloppy that it is difficult to make out a name. On other sherds the letters are remarkably neat and orderly, as if their authors were more comfortable with writing. This lack of uniformity is what characterizes most of the *ostraka* of K 2:7, and both this deposit and other Agora *ostraka* give every indication that *ostraka* were the work of individual Athenians scratching the names of candidates as best they could. Future finds may alter this impression, but for now the *ostraka* excavated in the Agora and elsewhere in Athens offer our best evidence for the basic level of literacy of Athenian citizens during the 5th century B.C.

THE ATHENIAN AGORA
EXCAVATIONS

A Pictorial History of the Agora Excavations

by Craig A. Mauzy

The Agora lies on sloping ground northwest of the Acropolis, the most conspicuous of the hills of Athens (Fig. 80). The extraordinarily well-preserved Doric Temple of Hephaistos, sometimes popularly known as the «Theseion» or «Hephaisteion», has always been visible on the hill to the west. The marble giants, reused as the facade of a Late Roman complex and the north end of the Stoa of Attalos, preserved to its full height, also remained evident through the centuries. The other ancient remains were not so well preserved, however, and their ruins lay as much as eight meters below the modern surface, covered from the 10th century A.D. by an extensive neighborhood of private houses. The houses were repeatedly rebuilt after successive invasions by Franks, Ottomans, and Venetians. The last destruction occurred in 1826, the result of a siege of the Acropolis during the Greek War of Independence.

Once again the neighborhood was totally rebuilt (Fig. 81) but only limited archaeological excavation was possible, due to the financial constraints of building the new nation. The Greek Archaeological Society cleared the Stoa of Attalos of debris in 1859–1862 and 1898–1902 (Fig. 82). The extension of the Athens–Piraeus railroad cut through the northern part of the site in 1890–1891 (Fig. 83). German and Greek archaeologists opened up other areas in 1896–1897 and 1907–1908 (Fig. 84). Except for these scattered and limited attempts, the remains of the center of ancient Athens lay deeply buried, inaccessible, and largely forgotten.

The challenges of excavation were considerable. The site had been occupied almost continuously for close to 5,000 years, so the stratigraphy was disturbed and complex. In addition, as well as sharing all the logistical problems inherent in any large-

Fig. 80
A view of Athens as seen from the slopes of Lykabettos Hill. Engraving titled «Athens from the Foot of Mount Anchesmus», from the book «Views in Greece from Drawings by Edward Dodwell», London 1821. Courtesy Gennadius Library Archives.

⇦ Fig. 81
A view looking north from the Acropolis showing the area of the Agora. The Temple of Hephaistos is clearly visible on the left and the crowded neighborhood built on top of the ancient Agora lies below. Photograph by Gabriel de Rumine, 1858, courtesy National Historical Museum of Athens, Photographic Archive.

⇦ Fig. 82
A view of the Stoa of Attalos taken in 1910 from the southwest corner of the building. This photograph was made considerably after the Greek Archaeological Society at Athens excavated the area in 1859–1862 and 1898–1902. Archaeological Society at Athens, Photographic Archive.

⇗ Fig. 83
A view of the construction of the Athens–Piraeus railway line that cut through the northern edge of the Agora in the mid-1880s. The photograph was taken from the intersection of Hadrian and Vrisakiou streets looking west. The northeast corner of the Stoa of Attalos can be seen on the left-hand side. Courtesy Gennadius Library Archives.

⇩ Fig. 84
A photograph of the German Archaeological Institute's excavations on the west side of the Agora just below the Hephaisteion, 1896. Courtesy German Archaeological Institute of Athens, Photographic Archive, Neg. D-DAI-ATH-Athen Bauten 126.

Fig. 85 Aerial view of the Agora excavations in 1933.

1. The railway at the top of the photograph defines the northern edge of the original excavations;

2. the Temple of Hephaistos and hill of Kolonos Agoraios define the western side;

3. the foundation of the Stoa of Attalos defines the eastern side;

4. the Areopagus hill forms the southern limit of the excavations.

scale urban excavation, the Agora site must be one of the few where a street (Hadrian Street), a railway, and a river (the Eridanos River) divide the area of the excavations (Fig 85).

The systematic excavation of the ancient Athenian Agora was entrusted by the Greek state to the American School of Classical Studies at the end of the 1920s. The area to be explored covered some 24 acres (nearly 10 hectares) and was occupied by 365 modern houses, all of which had to be purchased and demolished. T. Leslie Shear was appointed the first field director and assembled a staff that included some of the best-known names in Greek archaeology: Homer A. Thompson, Eugene Vanderpool,

Benjamin Meritt, Dorothy Burr (Thompson), Virginia Grace, Lucy Talcott, Alison Frantz, Piet de Jong, and John Travlos, among others.

After several years of preparation, the actual work of the excavations began in May 1931. Since then, hundreds of scholars, workers, specialists, and students have participated in the excavation, conservation, research, and publication of the site and its related finds. Collectively, they are responsible for one of the most productive archaeological projects in the Mediterranean basin. More than 50 volumes and hundreds of scholarly articles have been published, adding much to our understanding of all aspects of ancient Greek history and society.

A Picture of the Agora before Excavations Began

After Greece was reborn as a modern nation in 1830, increasing numbers of visitors began to arrive to see its ancient monuments firsthand. Some of these early travelers left written accounts while others drew or painted their impressions. Few accounts or descriptions exist of the area that overlay the ancient Agora, since it was largely buried beneath the successive layers of nearly 20 centuries of habitation. The Temple of Hephaistos and the «giants» (of the Roman Odeion) were still visible and glimpses of antiquities could be seen at some points in the surrounding neighborhood, but there was in general little indication of the wonders that lay below the surface.

An engraving of the Stoa of Attalos illustrates that the northeast corner of the building had survived intact all the way to its gable (Fig. 86). The Edward Dodwell drawing from which the engraving was made can be dated to 1805, when the artist was in Athens, two decades before the siege of the Acropolis. The devastation of the city caused during the War of Independence is captured in two watercolors by J. J. Wolfensberger dated to 1834. In the first, the artist has taken a position next to one of the «giants» in the center of the Agora (where excavations 100 years later would reveal the remains of the Roman Odeion) (Fig. 87). The second watercolor attributed to the same artist is from a vantage point slightly north of the «giants» (Fig. 88). Again, the Hephaisteion stands prominently in the center on the hill of Kolonos Agoraios and the ruins of houses show the devastation of the area.

In a letter written in 1834 by Richard Burgess to a friend, we read an account of what Athens looked like in the early 19th century. The letter describes the author's impression arriving in Piraeus Harbor, making his way to Athens, and coming upon his first glimpse of the ancient city.

↘ Fig. 86

Engraving of the northeast corner of the Stoa of Attalos. Titled «Ruins of the Gymnasium of Ptolemy at Athens», this was Plate 71 in «Views and Descriptions of Cyclopean or Pelasgic Remains in Greece and Italy with Constructions of a Later Period, from Drawings by the Late Edward Dodwell», London 1834. Compare this drawing to the nearly identical view in Figure 83. Courtesy Gennadius Library Archives.

⇐ Fig. 87

View looking west from the central area of the Agora with the Temple of Hephaistos in the background. J. J. Wolfensberger, 1834.

To John B. Scott, Esq., Bungay, Suffolk.
Athens, June 27, 1834

A very practicable road (not a common thing in Greece) leads through an olive grove to the city, which cannot be said to have either access or entrance in one place more than another. The most conspicuous object seen over all the plain is the Mount Anchesmus [Lykabettos hill]; next, the Acropolis, which is so familiar to every one's eyes, from drawings, that it cannot be mistaken. The other which at once arrests the eye is the Temple of Theseus [Temple of Hephaistos]. The walls which encircled the Athens of the Turks are now so nearly leveled with the ground, that the city at present cannot be said to have any assigned space; and it would, I conceive, be difficult for former travelers now to recognize, upon the spot, their own descriptions of what Athens was: but it is fortunate for the antiquary, that all the space between the Acropolis and the Illissus has been kept clear of buildings; and perhaps we are indebted to a Turkish cemetery for the veneration which has been shown to the Areopagus and the Pnyx by those who knew not why they should respect them. It is in the unpeopled valley, which lies beneath the hill of Museum [Philopappou Hill], where the genius of ancient Athens meets the stranger, and where he may wander undisturbed among «Fields that cool Ilissus laves». The desolation caused by the siege of 1827 is yet for the most part, unrepaired; whole streets lie prostrate in the dust, and beaten paths are made over the heaps of rubbish which point out the site of a Turkish bath, or the Serai of an Aga: but at a distance from the ruined habitations, and on the higher ground nearest the Acropolis, which is destined, I conceive, to become the most eligible part of Athens, you see large houses, reared here and there, indicating the return of wealth and peace if not authority.

Fig. 88
View of the west side of the Agora and the Temple of Hephaistos. Attributed to J. J. Wolfensberger, 1834.

The Earliest Photographs

In 1839, just five years after J. J. Wolfensberger painted his watercolors of the Agora, the discovery of the daguerreotype process was announced in Paris. The patent for the process, the first practical method to capture and fix an image on a photosensitive surface, was subsequently acquired by the French government and presented free to its citizens as a way to encourage development in the arts and sciences. Describing the new procedure to members of the Academy of Sciences and Fine Arts, the chemist François Arago pointed out the benefit to the field of archaeology: «To copy the thousands of hieroglyphs that cover the great monuments of Thebes, Memphis, Karnak, would require a score of years and legions of draftsmen. With the daguerreotype, one man alone can carry out this immense work, without errors». Travelers making the Grand Tour of Italy, Greece, Egypt, and the Levant quickly realized how useful the new invention would be for capturing images of the monuments and sites they were to visit. Just months after the process was announced, Pierre-Gaspard-Gustave Joly de Lotbiniere, preparing for a Grand Tour, obtained the necessary equipment to make daguerreotypes and set off on his journey. He arrived in Athens in October, proceeded to the Acropolis, and captured an image of the Parthenon in 1839, perhaps the first photograph of an archaeological monument in Greece. Although the original daguerreotype does not exist, a copy of the image along with others was published in the book *Excursions daguerriennes: Vues et monuments les plus remarquables du globe* (Paris 1841–1842).

In 1842, another Frenchman, Joseph-Philibert Girault de Prangey, also set off with the new invention. A well-educated gentleman scholar of his time, Girault de Prangey had spent the decade prior to his departure exploring Spain and had studied its Moorish architecture, recording what he saw with drawings. Perhaps this experience convinced him of the practical advantage of using the daguerreotype over traditional means of recording with pen and ink. His journey would last three years as he traveled throughout the Mediterranean producing nearly 1,000 daguerreotypes of its most important ancient monuments, including approximately 70 images in Athens. One of the images is particularly significant for the history of photography of Greece as it is the oldest known surviving daguerreotype of the most conspicuous monument in Athens, the Acropolis. Taken in 1842 from the square south of the Hephaisteion, Girault de Prangey captured a view of the entire Acropolis and its northern slopes covered with houses (Fig. 89). Of particular inter-

Fig. 89
View of the Acropolis and houses on its north slope, 1842. Two identical images have been exposed on the same copper plate so it appears as if one is floating above the other. The daguerreotype process reverses the scene resulting in a mirror image. The viewer in this instance is given the false impression of looking at the Acropolis from the south. In fact these daguerreotypes were made at the same location as Fig. 90, next to the Temple of Hephaistos. Daguerreotype by Joseph-Philibert Girault de Prangey, courtesy Gernsheim Collection, Harry Ransom Humanities Research Center, University of Texas at Austin.

est for the pictorial history of the Agora is that this image preserves the oldest photographic view of the neighborhood that overlay the ancient Agora.

The realistic rendering and extraordinary detail of scenes captured by these Frenchmen and others soon to follow heralded a new way of experiencing the monuments. An individual no longer had to visit the monuments personally, but could experience them through photographic images. The circulation and publication of these images helped stimulate interest in the ancient civilizations. More travelers followed, and some were to become early pioneers of the developing field of professional photography in Greece.

John Shaw Smith, an Irishman interested in archaeology and ancient history, was one of these early pioneers of photography. Smith embarked on the Grand Tour in 1850 with his wife. He used the calotype process to make his photographs, a process that was being developed in England at the same time the daguerreotype process was being developed in France. A calotype is made through a two-step method. The original image is captured on a paper negative and then a positive print is made. The pro-

cess rapidly became the preferred method of taking photographs, quickly gaining popularity after paper negatives were replaced by glass negatives, and is the direct ancestor of analog photography that uses film. Smith's contribution to the technique was that he successfully adapted the process for use in hot climates and brought back more than 300 images of his travels. A photograph made by him in 1850 standing next to the Hephaisteion with his camera pointed toward the Acropolis preserves another early image of the neighborhood that covered the ancient Agora (Fig. 90).

During the last decades of the 19th century some photographers began to recognize that photographs of ancient monuments could be sold as souvenirs to visitors, while others began producing photographic albums for sale abroad. For students and scholars studying classical antiquity who had no possibility of visiting the archaeological sites themselves, examining photographs was almost as good as being there. Notable topographical images of Athens were created by Filippos Margaritis, Felix Bonfils, and the Romaidis brothers (Fig. 91).

Fig. 90
Calotype photograph by John Shaw Smith, 1850. Taken looking from the Temple of Hephaistos toward the Acropolis (almost an identical view as that shown in Figure 89, although this photograph is correctly oriented). The houses on the north slope that covered the ancient Agora and the Frankish tower on the Acropolis are clearly visible.

Documenting the Excavations

As photography developed, archaeologists soon came to recognize the value of taking photographs while the excavation was in progress. Whereas an excavator's written description and observations may be perceived as subjective, photography provides an objective record. In addition, photographs capture a wealth of information quickly and succinctly, giving proof of the adage «a picture is worth a thousand words».

Comparing an excavation to a crime scene is a useful analogy that emphasizes how vigilant in preserving the archaeological record an archaeologist must be. Just as a detective gathers evidence that may be used in a trial, an archaeologist collects evidence that forms the basis of future scholarship. Just as evidence at a crime scene can easily be lost, the features of an excavation are constantly changing and can vanish if not recorded (Figs. 92 and 93).

Excavating an archaeological site is essentially a destructive process. To document the process, archaeologists keep notebooks in which they describe

their observations in words, make drawings, and place photographs (Fig. 94). Recording the context of where an object was found or feature was uncovered is crucial to the evidentiary value of the object or feature itself. Photographs provide significant corroborating evidence because they were taken during the excavation and the documentation of when and where they were made is key to their value. The notebook preserves the factual evidence observed by the archaeologist. The objects and photographs preserve supporting evidence critical to understanding the archaeological record.

As objects are recovered, the metaphor of the excavation as a crime scene extends to how objects are processed by archaeologists. Just as suspects are «booked» at a police station, objects are registered the moment they are discovered and before their removal from the ground. A number is assigned, providing a unique identity for the object, and this number is essential for keeping track of all the information that pertains to the artifact as it moves

Fig. 91
Panoramic view of Athens from the Hill of the Observatory, made by Felix Bonfils in 1873. The Temple of Hephaistos is visible low down to the left; the Acropolis is on the right; between these monuments lies the area of the Agora, covered by houses. Lykabettos hill is shown in the center. Courtesy Evi Antonatos Collection.

Fig. 92
The discovery of a marble statue of the Winged Nike (S 312) from the Stoa of Zeus, 1933. The archaeologist is examining and technicians cleaning the statue; baskets filled with pottery are visible.

Fig. 93
Three views of excavation section Z taken from the same
vantage point illustrate the progress of the excavation over a
two-month period in 1933.

from excavation through conservation and is finally
catalogued. From the very first season of American
excavations at the Athenian Agora, a catalogue system was used to register objects. When the object arrived for cataloguing, an inventory number was assigned depending on the class of objects to which it
belonged, such as sculpture, pottery, lamps, and so
on. A full description of the object was then typed on
an index card along with the object's storage information. A photograph was taken and a contact print
of the negative glued to the card for quick reference
(Fig. 95). Lucy Talcott, who worked at the Agora
from 1933 to 1958, is credited with developing the
card catalogue into an elaborate cross-referenced
recording system. The catalogue card became the
most important repository of all the relevant data
concerning an object and has only recently been replaced by a digital database, as described further in
Chapter 11.

Some of the earliest images found in the Agora's
photographic archive were taken by the photographer M. Messinessi and are dated to early 1930
(Fig. 96). The first director of the excavations,
T. Leslie Shear, commissioned Messinessi to document the area of the Agora for the permanent record. Although the original intention of the photographs was to scientifically document the topmost
layer of the archaeological record, they are of great
social interest as well. Caught in the photographs
are views of one Athenian neighborhood (of people,
domestic life, buildings, and details of architecture)
at just the point when the urban landscape of Athens was beginning to change rapidly. The practice
of documenting «before» views continues to the
present, and after 75 years an important collection of photographs has grown and is a valuable
resource for anyone interested in the modern
history of Athens.

Hermann Wagner was the first photographer to work
as a staff member of the Agora excavations. His first
photograph was made standing at the northeast corner
of the Temple of Hephaistos on May 25, 1931, when

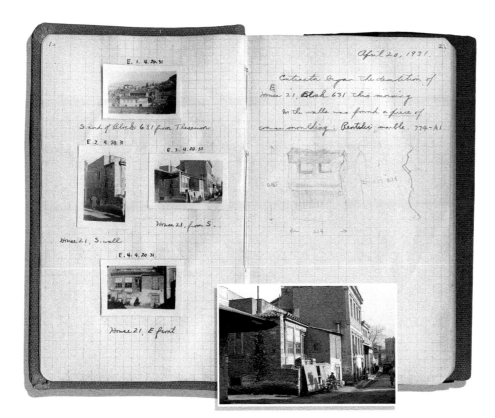

Fig. 94
Pages of the first notebook for section E. The first building to be demolished, house 21-631, is illustrated in the enlarged photograph. The discovery of a small architectural fragment found in a wall during demolition is recorded in the notebook.

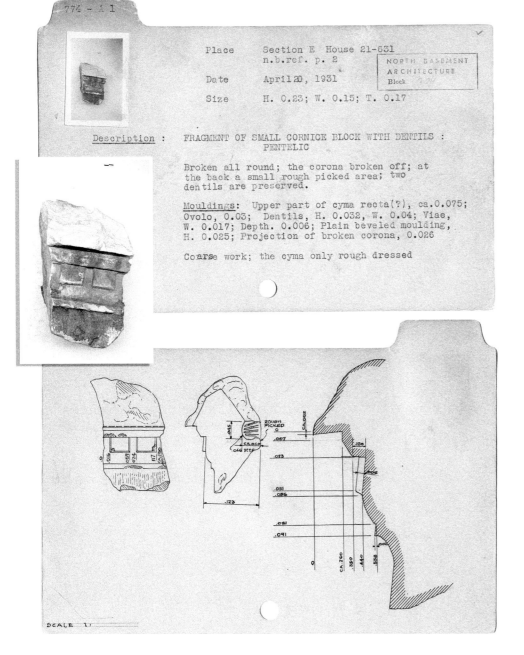

Fig. 95
The catalogue card, front and back, of A 1, the first architectural piece to be catalogued (recorded in the notebook entry shown in Figure 94). The date and place where the object was found, with a brief description and its general dimensions, were noted by the archaeologist and recorded in the notebook. Later, a fuller description was made and transferred to the catalogue card after the object had passed through conservation and was formally accessioned by a curator. A photograph, for quick reference, is glued to the card.

Fig. 96
The intersection of Asteroskopeiou and Apollodorous streets, taken by M. Messinessi in 1930. This is one of a collection of some 90 photographs commissioned by T. Leslie Shear to record the area of the Agora before excavations began.

Fig. 97
Section E, the first area to be explored, May 25, 1931. In the foreground is the area previously investigated by Greek and German archaeologists; beyond the wall, workmen are excavating in front of the Church of Panagia Vlassarou.

↗ Fig. 98
Section E taken from the Church of Panagia Vlassarou on the first day of excavations, May 25, 1931, looking west. The Temple of Hephaistos is in the background.

⇧ Fig. 99
Photograph shot using a Leica camera by a 1930s excavator. The photograph provides a candid view of work on the excavations.

work in the first section began (Fig. 97). Wagner, associated with the German Archaeological Institute for some years, was an experienced archaeological photographer and established high professional standards for the Agora excavations from the very beginning. He shot nearly 2,500 negatives during the eight years he worked at the Agora excavations. Most of his images are outdoor views but Wagner also made photographs of the first objects to be recovered that were destined for publication. Wagner's camera produced large 18 cm x 24 cm negatives that captured an astonishing wealth of detail (Fig. 98).

An innovation that the Agora excavation team brought to archaeological photography was the introduction of the Leica, a small handheld 35 mm camera. The Leica permitted the excavators to create quick visual records for themselves as well as capturing candid views of the work on the excavations that bring the process to life for modern viewers. The 35 mm outdoor excavation photographs and the large-format images made by the staff photographer complement each other and are both integral to the photographic record of the excavations (Fig. 99).

In 1934, Alison Frantz came to the Agora to assist Lucy Talcott with the catalogue system. An interest in photography was rekindled and she began taking pictures of the objects for the card catalogue. While Frantz completed her doctorate during the next few years she gradually increased her mastery of photography. When Wagner departed in 1939, Frantz was selected to replace him and she continued working at the Agora until 1964. As a scholar she was to make significant contributions to the study of late antiquity in Greece while also working at the Agora as photographer (Fig. 100).

For most people, the glamorous and exciting side of archaeological photography is working in the field, photographing the discoveries while they are being made. The less glamorous but equally important part of work at an excavation is the object photography necessary for cataloguing the objects and for publication (Fig. 101). Practically speaking, the quantity of object photographs far exceeds the number of outdoor photographs.

Initially an object photograph serves to identify the object for cataloguing purposes, much as a «mug shot» identifies an individual who has been arrested. The object is photographed so that im-

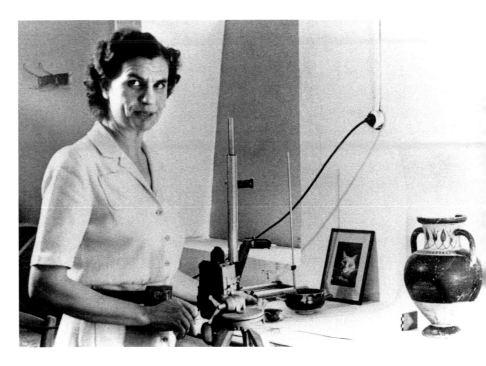

Fig. 100
Alison Frantz in her studio using a Leica camera to photograph objects for the card catalogue, 1947.

Fig. 101
The archaeologist Rodney Young sorting pottery fragments from a well (deposit A 17:2), 1947.

Fig. 102
Two views of a bronze head of a Nike (B 30). The left photograph was shot immediately after the piece was found in 1932 but before cleaning. The right photograph was taken using a digital camera in 2007.

B 30

portant identifying details are brought out, often against a white background so that its shape is easily recognized and including a scale to provide a sense of size. Conventions have been established so that classes of objects are photographed in a similar way, making comparisons between different objects easy. When an object is to be published, a more thorough photographic record is often made to include top, bottom, and profile views and other relevant details (Fig. 102).

The First Years of Excavation: 1931–1940

Exploration of the ancient Athenian Agora began on May 25, 1931. Nearly all of the Agora we see today was uncovered during the 10 prewar excavation seasons, working in four- to five-month periods, often with more than 100 workmen.

Initially excavations were concentrated on the west side at the base of the hill, Kolonos Agoraios, where most of the important civic buildings and monuments of the Classical city were found (Fig. 103). The Monument of the Eponymous Heroes was discovered during the first season. The Stoa of Zeus, the Metroon, the Bouleuterion, and the Tholos, buildings that define the western side of the square, were discovered in subsequent years. Crowning Kolonos Agoraios is the Temple of Hephaistos around which investigations revealed evidence of a garden, metalworking, and ceramic manufacture (Fig. 104). The central area of the Agora as far north as the railway tracks was explored and a corner of the Altar of the Twelve Gods was found. In the center, the Temple of Ares and the Odeion were uncovered. Farther south, at the base of the Areopagus, the remains of two large stoas and two fountains were excavated, defining the southern limit of the ancient square (Fig. 105). A road cutting diagonally across the excavations from the northwest to southeast was identified as the Panathenaic Way. Investigations continued eastward to the foundations of the Stoa of Attalos and defined the eastern limit of the ancient Agora (Fig. 106).

The so-called Old Excavation House located at Asteroskopeiou Street 25, was actually a group of houses and formed a complex of temporary storerooms and workspace for the early excavations. All of the antiquities that had been found to date were stored in these buildings. Planning for the construction of a museum to properly display the important pieces and to house the enormous quantity of excavated material had already begun by 1939, but all work at the excavation was suspended in the spring of 1940 due to the start of World War II.

The 1939 excavation season was the last full season of fieldwork at the Agora before World War II. A brief five-week excavation season was conducted in 1940, but most attention was devoted to preparing for the possibility that Greece would be drawn into the war. Protective measures were taken to pack

Fig. 103
The staff and workmen of the 1933 excavation season sitting in front of the Temple of Hephaistos on the eastern slope of the hill of Kolonos Agoraios.

the finds and the excavation records in bombproof shelters after duplicate records had been made and sent to America. The more valuable pieces were boxed and given over to the Greek authorities for safekeeping.

Fig. 104
Excavations on the slopes of the hill of Kolonos Agoraios just below the Temple of Hephaistos, 1932. This section joined the area excavated by the Greek and German archaeologists in the late 1800s.

Fig. 105
Standing with the Acropolis to his back, the photographer captured a view of excavations in 1933 of the southeast corner of the Agora. In the center of the photograph, running top to bottom (north to south), is a Late Roman fortification wall and to the right are foundations of the Stoa of Attalos.

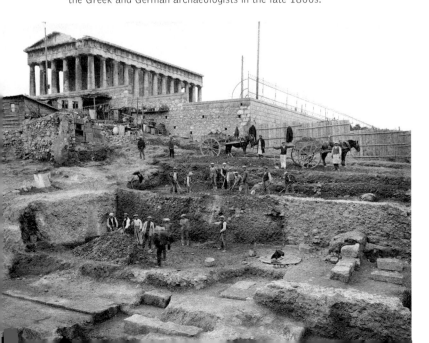

Excavation Work Resumes: 1946–1956

Work on the Agora resumed in the spring of 1946 under the leadership of Homer A. Thompson, replacing T. Leslie Shear, who had died suddenly the year before. Thompson was named field director the following year and would keep that position until his retirement in 1967. Thompson's immediate attention was devoted to fulfilling two pledges made by the American School when it began excavations and a third commitment the School took on itself. Thus for the next 10 years, in addition to continued excavations throughout the Agora to finish work interrupted by the war, Thompson's energies were dedicated to the reconstruction of the Stoa of Attalos, the restoration of the Church of the Holy Apostles, and the creation of an archaeological park.

Fig. 106
Panoramic view of the excavations in 1936, prepared by scanning three photographs taken from the roof of the Temple of Hephaistos and joining them using software.

Fig. 107
View of the foundations of the Stoa of Attalos, November 1952. The building was rebuilt between 1953 and 1956. Where possible, remains of the ancient building were incorporated. The northern end preserved to the roof line is visible on the left side of the picture.

The Reconstruction of the Stoa of Attalos

Fig. 108
View of the progress of reconstructing the Stoa of Attalos, April 1956.

Fig. 109
View of the finished reconstructed Stoa of Attalos, December 1956.

The Stoa of Attalos was originally built by King Attalos II of Pergamon (159–138 B.C.) as a gift to the Athenians in appreciation of the time he had spent in Athens studying under the philosopher Karneades. What he gave the city was an elaborate stoa, a large two-storey double colonnade with rows of shops behind the colonnades, made of local materials: marble for the facade and columns and limestone for the walls. As the major commercial building or shopping center in the Agora, the Stoa of Attalos was used for centuries, from its construction ca. 150 B.C. until its destruction at the hands of the Herulians in A.D. 267. The decision to reconstruct the building as the museum was made because it was large enough and because enough architectural elements were preserved to allow an accurate reconstruction. The northern end even stood to the original roof line, allowing precision in recreating the height of the building.

The Stoa of Attalos was rebuilt between 1953 and 1956. Where possible, remains of the original building were incorporated: the north end, the southernmost shops, part of the south wall, and the south end of the outer steps (Fig. 107). Elsewhere the modern reconstruction rests on the original foundations and is an almost exact replica of the ancient building, with representative pieces of the original included to allow the visitor a chance to check the validity of the reconstruction. Quarries in Piraeus and on Mt. Penteli were opened to provide material similar to the original. As many as 150 workmen were employed, including 50 master masons, 20 carpenters, and 5 steelworkers (Fig. 108).

Dedicated on September 3, 1956, the Stoa of Attalos celebrated its 50th anniversary as the Agora museum in 2006. The ground floor is given over to public display. Sculpture and large architectural marbles are exhibited in the colonnades. Smaller objects are displayed in a long gallery consisting of 10 of the original shops on the ground floor. The top floor is used for the excavation offices, workrooms, and archives as well as for additional storage. More storerooms were created in a basement constructed beneath the original foundations.

Fig. 110
View of the narthex of the Church of the Holy Apostles with
wooden scaffolding constructed to erect the domes, February
1955. Though several churches were removed in the clearing
of the site for excavation, it was decided to save and restore this
little Byzantine church, which is among the oldest in Athens,
probably to be dated just before A.D. 1000.

The reconstruction leads the visitor to appreciate why stoas were such a common form of public building among the Greeks, used in agoras and sanctuaries, near theaters, and wherever many people were expected to gather. The spacious colonnades provided shelter for literally thousands of people, protecting them from sun in summer and wind and rain in winter, while allowing in abundant light and fresh air (Fig. 109).

⇩ Fig. 111
View of the Church of the Holy Apostles after restoration, October 1957.

The Church of the Holy Apostles

Though several churches were removed in the clearing of the site for excavation, it was decided to save and restore the little Byzantine church dedicated to the Holy Apostles. The church, with an unusual interior plan and decorative tile work on the exterior, is among the oldest in Athens, probably to be dated just before A.D. 1000. It was surely the focal point of an extensive neighborhood in the Byzantine period, the remains of which were recorded and removed in the course of the excavations. The eastern half of the church was relatively untouched, but several additions, the latest dating to the late 19th century, had damaged and obscured the western end. After excavation, these later additions were removed and the church was restored to its original form (Fig. 110). The work was funded by the Samuel H. Kress Foundation and supervised by Alison Frantz. With the Stoa of Attalos, this restoration was completed and dedicated in 1956 (Fig. 111). The festival of the Twelve Apostles is still celebrated at the church every June 30th.

Landscaping the Agora

As part of the same project to restore the Stoa of Attalos and the Church of the Holy Apostles, the entire archaeological site was landscaped and planted in the 1950s in order to turn the excavated area into an archaeological park. A guiding principle was to use plants native to Greece and in particular those known to have been available in antiquity. One instance of ancient planting around the Hephaisteion, recovered by excavation, led to the planting of two rows of bushes — one of pomegranates, the second of myrtle — around the old temple. In all, more than 4,500 trees, shrubs, and vines were planted in an effort to render the site more inviting to the visitor and to provide the city of Athens with much-needed parkland. Paths, benches, and labels for the monuments were also part of the landscaping program (Fig. 112).

Fig. 112
Before and after photographs of the landscaping project and the transformation of the excavations into an archaeological park. The photograph above was taken in 1937, the one below in 2005. Both views are taken from just below the Temple of Hephaistos looking across the site toward the Stoa of Attalos.

A Period of Consolidation: 1956–1967

Work at the Agora from 1956 until 1967 can be characterized as a period of consolidating the archaeological evidence. The main focus during this period was the study and publication of the vast amount of material that had been uncovered (Fig. 113). In the field, limited excavations continued throughout the site to conclude earlier explorations. Indoors, the staff worked closely with scholars to prepare for publication 10 additional volumes in the Athenian Agora monograph series. Small guides to the site and its antiquities were published to help visitors understand and appreciate the newly created archaeological park and its unique history. The Agora Picture Book series still continues, and electronic copies can be downloaded from the Agora Web site (http://www.agathe.gr).

During this period of intense study and examination of the archaeological record, the staff came to recognize that the northern edge of the Agora had not yet been revealed and that several important buildings remained elusively unaccounted for. Sometimes the identity of a building or monument was immediately known by the fortunate discovery of an inscription, but often archaeologists had to rely on the rich literary sources from ancient texts to help identify the buildings, especially the account left by the Roman traveler Pausanias, who visited the Agora around A.D. 150.

His account, which describes a walking tour of the Agora starting from the Dipylon gate, the entrance to the city from the Kerameikos, helped substantiate the location of many buildings. It also, however, mentioned two important buildings that were still missing from the archaeological discoveries. These (the Royal Stoa and the Painted Stoa) must, according to Pausanias's description, lie north of the railway line, a modern boundary that had been built in the 1880s and arbitrarily divided the ancient Athenian Agora.

Fig. 113
Margaret Crosby examining architectural pieces she was preparing for publication, left; Eugene Vanderpool studying the Phrynichos Stele (I 6524), May 1952, right.

Finding the Missing Buildings: 1968–1978

T. Leslie Shear Jr., son of the first field director, was appointed director of the excavations in 1968. The following year, excavations began in the narrow strip of land that lay north of the existing excavations but south of Hadrian Street. In 1970, a small stoa was discovered squeezed between the railway tracks and Hadrian Street. The building that

Fig. 114
An aerial photograph from 1975 shows section BΓ, where the Royal Stoa was discovered: (1) the Royal Stoa, squeezed between the railway tracks and Hadrian Street; (2) a length of the partially covered Great Drain; (3) the Crossroads Enclosure; (4) the Panathenaic Way; and (5) the north/south road on the western side of the Agora. This aerial photograph is one from a series taken by J. Wilson and Ellie Myers for the Agora excavations. A balloon carried aloft a camera whose shutter was then triggered by radio control to make the exposure.

Fig. 115
The mass of pottery dating to the 5th century B.C. found in the Crossroads Enclosure.

Fig. 116
Section BΔ, the area to be excavated between the railway and Hadrian Street, with modern houses removed, 1969.

Fig. 117
Aerial view of section
BΔ after excavation, 1975:
(1) the foundation of a
basilica; (2) a Roman
house; (3) the columns
and tile roof of the Stoa
of Attalos; and (4) the
modern street and houses
that obviously cover more
of the ancient city.

was later conclusively identified as the Royal Stoa was found just north of the Stoa of Zeus (Fig. 114). Its location precisely matched Pausanias's description. Exploration of the area to the east of the Royal Stoa revealed layer upon layer of stratigraphy of the Panathenaic Way at the point where it turns into the Agora. The intersection of the Panathenaic Way and the road running north to south along the west side of the Agora was investigated and an enclosed shrine and well were discovered. A substantial number of votive objects, mostly of pottery, were recovered from both the crossroads shrine and the well (Fig. 115). Explorations continued further east, partially revealing the foundations of a large basilica and a house but still no evidence of the other missing stoa (Figs. 116 and 117).

The Current Phase of Exploration: 1980–Present

In 1980, excavations began north of Hadrian Street, initiating the current phase of explorations of the Agora. The year also marked the inauguration of a new approach to the excavation of the Agora. Under the supervision of archaeologists and members of our staff, student volunteers are trained to excavate (Fig. 118). The purpose of this approach, which still continues, is to give students the opportunity to work on an excavation and introduce them to archaeological methods through practical experience.

During the 1981 season, two discoveries were made that confirmed the need to excavate north of Hadrian Street. Propitiously, a herm was found early in the season, adding to the large number already recovered from the northwest corner of the Agora. More significant still was the discovery a few weeks later of a corner of a large finely made building. Subsequent investigation uncovered the western end of a stoa that measured 12.5 meters wide. Recent discoveries indicate the length of the stoa to be at least 48 meters. This stoa can be dated to around 475 B.C. from pottery found associated with its construction.

⇦ Fig. 118
An aerial view of the excavations, 1982. Outlines of the major features and monuments help the viewer understand the complexity of the site. Starting at the top: (1) the area of current excavations; (2) the probable outline of the Painted Stoa; (3) the Royal Stoa; (4) the Crossroads Enclosure; (5) the Stoa of Zeus; (6) the road along the west side; and (7) a section of the course of the Panathenaic Way.

Given its size and location, this building is almost certainly the Painted Stoa, the other missing stoa mentioned by Pausanias (Fig. 119). Further excavations to the west revealed the fine marble base of an altar and the foundation of a large Roman building, possibly a bath.

John McK. Camp II was appointed director of the excavations in 1994. Camp has supervised the continued enlargement of the area of exploration as far north as Astingos (Hastings) Street and east to St. Phillip's Street. Gradually, as buildings, walls, and objects have been uncovered it has become apparent

Fig. 119
The west end of the probable Painted Stoa just after its discovery, 1981. The identification of the building is based on its size and location, which match the descriptions of the Roman traveler Pausanias.

Fig. 120
Excavations in section BH during the 2007 season. Byzantine features have been uncovered nearly 3 m beneath the basements of the demolished buildings. Walkways have been built to cart away the earth. Baskets and buckets are filled with pottery and an umbrella provides shade for the excavators.

that the character of the neighborhood north of the Painted Stoa changed over time. A street originating next to the Painted Stoa begins at the Panathenaic Way and leads to the northwest. It is bordered on the east by buildings of definite commercial use, and on the west by a Roman bath. It seems clear from the archaeological record that the Painted Stoa forms the northern limit of the Agora, the civic center of ancient Athens. Three modern buildings have been demolished recently, enlarging the area of exploration, which will permit nearly all of the Painted Stoa to be uncovered in the coming years (Fig. 120).

If we accept Pausanias's account and other literary sources that have proven to be remarkably accurate, another stoa, known as the Stoa of the Herms, remains to be discovered in the northwest corner of the Agora. The large number of herms recovered in the vicinity supports the hypothesis that this missing stoa will be found nearby. It seems likely that it lies to the west of the present excavations. The difficulty and cost of excavating in an urban environment discourages speculation about how soon it may be found. Perhaps future generations of archaeologists will be inspired to find it by developing new techniques of exploration that preserve the contemporary city above while examining the ancient one below.

From Pot-Mending to Conservation: An Art Becomes a Science

by Amandina Anastassiades

In antiquity, as today, artifacts were broken or lost through natural disasters, war, vandalism, theft, or simple individual carelessness. Once forgotten, personal and public effects are buried over time along with other physical remains of human habitation. Even if an object during its useful life is fortunate enough to survive an array of natural and human influences intact, its chances of then surviving burial undamaged are very small. The condition, as well as the type of finds uncovered from a site, entirely depends on the makeup of the ground in which the object rests: humidity, temperature, oxygen, pollution, pH, and the presence of salts in the soil all play a role. At the Athenian Agora, soil traits are optimal for the general preservation of vessels and figurines fashioned from clay, as well as sculptures, inscriptions, and grave markers chiseled from stone. The soil is somewhat suitable for preserving coins, tools, weapons, and jewelry cast and forged from metals; and the survival of human and animal skeletal remains is quite good. In contrast, the environment is poor for preserving textiles, wood, and other artifacts made from organic materials, and these are uncovered only on rare occasions.

Once recovered from the ground by archaeologists, finds are entrusted to conservators who clean away the dirt, piece together the fragments, and ensure the artifacts' long-term preservation. Conserving archaeological materials has developed from an art into a science. In the early days, those who bore the responsibility were known as pot-menders and their line of work was restoration. Today, the profession is known as conservation and those practicing it are conservators.

The Stoa of Attalos, located in the Agora, is home to the excavation's repository, archive, muse-

um, and workplace. The reconstructed 2nd-century B.C. building currently houses around 160,000 artifacts and roughly 230 cubic meters of context material. It is here, in this unique environment where all excavation documentation is stored on the ancient site, that Agora conservators work year round with the records personnel, an architect, a resident artist, and photographers to prepare the collections for archaeologists and visiting scholars to study and publish.

Fig. 121

Handles and much of the body of this vessel were restored in painted plaster by the pot-menders employed by the Agora excavations in the early years. Although acceptable at the time, this degree of reconstruction would be seen as excessive by professional conservators today.

Pot-Menders: The Early Years (1931–1980)

During the early days, excavations in the Athenian Agora lasted four to five months a year, with a handful of archaeologists and sometimes more than 100 workers moving up to 10,000 tons of earth in a season. The number of finds uncovered was equally staggering, and the task of preparing artifacts for study fell largely to the aptly named pot-menders. Although ceramics consumed most of their time, pot-menders were generally responsible for preserving all artifacts recovered from a site.

Like many pot-menders employed by foreign excavations, those of the Agora were local, self-taught, talented artisans. In the early days, returning artifacts as close as possible to their original form was the common practice. Equipped with few resources, the work of Agora menders equaled international standards of the time as they used many of the same techniques and materials employed by restorers in the major museums of Europe and North America. An Agora mender had to have a keen eye, excellent manual skills, and a sense of artistic expression. In certain individuals, artistic ability was combined with self-taught basic knowledge of chemistry, physics, and engineering.

Working closely with archaeologists and other scholars, restorers recreated whole artifacts from excavated fragments. Over time, menders replicated missing elements without guidance and thus became heavily responsible for interpreting and forming many of the missing sections, restorations that are still intact and on display today (Fig. 121). The menders' old restorations can now be seen as historical pieces in themselves, attesting to the chapter in archaeology when the restorers' finished product was expected to resemble the original, complete object.

Fig. 122 (left) Watercolor of a red-figure amphora showing Nike and a charioteer by Piet de Jong, the archaeological illustrator who worked at the Athenian Agora from the 1930s until 1962. Areas of restoration are carefully shown, but this image shows only one side of the artifact and thus does not reveal the whole history of restoration.

Fig. 123 (right) A pot-mender at work in the Old Excavation House, before the excavation headquarters moved to the Stoa of Attalos.

Piet de Jong, the Agora's chief artist during the early years of the excavation (ca. 1931—1962), depicted, at least in part, some of the menders' work in color. De Jong completed approximately 300 watercolor illustrations of excavated finds. In his paintings he accurately copied restored areas as faithfully as original sections (Fig. 122). As with the photocatalogue archive, however, de Jong usually painted only the most complete view of an artifact. Early photographs and watercolors do not systematically document which parts of most artifacts were original and which were restored.

A handful of candid black-and-white photographs show Agora menders laboring in their workshops surrounded by artifacts partially reconstructed and restored. Set amidst this landscape of vessels, the photos offer a glimpse of early restorations in progress, attesting to the vast volume of work faced by the menders and the central role they played in facilitating the study of archaeology (Fig. 123).

As seen in the photographs, mending archaeological finds requires time and plenty of space. Before the reconstruction of the Stoa of Attalos, restoration was undertaken in a group of houses that lay to the south of the Agora. The sign on the door of the mending area read *synkoleterion*, literally, «the place where things are glued together». Completion of the Stoa in 1956 established a permanent workspace for pot-mending — a spacious room on the upper tier.

Conservation Today (1980–Present)

Up to the late 1970s, pot-mending materials and treatments remained virtually unchanged at the Agora. By the late 1970s, however, professional bodies of conservators had formed in North America and Europe and international conservation practice standards had been established on both continents through university training programs and a body of literature that included professional codes of ethics. With the passing of the excavation's last chief pot-mender, Spyros Spyropoulos (Fig. 124), the first formally trained conservator was hired in 1980, and a new approach to caring for archaeological collections was introduced to the Agora.

The principal aspect that distinguishes conservation from the old pot-mending practice is record-keeping. Conservators document every stage of an artifact's care, whether it is being lifted from the ground or re-treated from storage. This record is extremely important for two reasons: the nature of conservation leads to removing information that, if not documented, may be lost forever; and treatments can fail with time, and it is easier for a conservator to remove or reverse an old treatment if the method and materials are known.

After documentation, the first step of a conservation treatment is examination. With the aid of microscopes, chemical tests, and analytical equipment, conservators carefully study each find for evidence or clues that provide information on the artifact's history and present condition. Conservators are able to distinguish whether a Roman bead is manufactured from glass or a semiprecious stone, a statuette of Aphrodite is carved from bone or ivory, a white pigment decorating a Classical vessel is made from chalk or lead, or a corroded copper alloy dagger had been wrapped in a sheath. In doing so, conservators play a key role in characterizing ancient materials and manufacturing techniques.

During cleaning, more time now is spent examining the corrosion and even dirt associated with finds from burial, as information for the archaeological record can be gained through careful investigation of these extraneous materials. Through painstaking observation, conservators at the Agora recently revealed the possible remains of ancient textiles covering a paint palette discovered in a Classical well and a Mycenaean jar found in a tomb. The evidence lies in the texture and form of the soil itself. In agreement with the archaeologists, the conservators left the dirt undisturbed and recorded it as part of the objects.

During examination, the structural and physical condition of the artifact is also assessed and weak points such as cracks, corrosion, and missing elements and the presence of substances harmful to the find, often acquired during burial, are identified.

These factors (the materials, the manufacturing techniques, and the condition) are not only of interest to the archaeologists but also affect the course and choice of the artifact's conservation treatment. In the 1980s and 1990s, Agora conservators illustrated how chemical and electrochemical treatments, used in the past to reduce disfiguring crusts or corrosion products from burial, actually removed original material or were detrimental to the long-term preservation of the finds. Based on this work and similar studies carried out at other institutions, simple mechanical cleaning techniques have largely replaced many chemical-based cleaning methods.

Following cleaning, fragmentary artifacts are reconstructed. Like a puzzle, pieces are organized and joined together. Shellac and other natural glues used for reconstructing finds in the early days, at the Agora and elsewhere, have now darkened and in many cases have failed. Today, these old adhesives have been almost completely abandoned by conservators for reconstructing archaeological finds and replaced with clear synthetic resins chosen for their long-term stability, reversibility, and aesthetic appearance.

Restoration, as opposed to reconstruction, is the process of filling or replicating missing sections with new materials. A full restoration can help scholars determine the original appearance of an object. These are rarely carried out, however, as the variety of objects that were manufactured in the ancient world is now well known and can often be deduced even from the smallest of fragments. Moreover, the scholarly community currently considers full restorations at risk of being interpretive and based on assumptions that can be misleading or inaccurate, which illustrates the value of being able to reverse the restoration process.

Restorations at the Agora are thus currently employed for structural purposes only — that is, to hold actual joining but unstable fragments together so that existing profiles can be drawn, photographed, and published. As scholars no longer require artifacts to look whole or complete, restoration materials and methods have changed. In the past, restoring large missing sections sometimes entailed providing extra support for heavy or cumbersome fills by applying generous amounts of plaster to the interior, underside, or back of the artifact. Frequently, supporting plaster was bulked or reinforced with available odds and ends such as metal netting, cotton wool, wax, or shellac — even empty cigarette packets have been discovered! The outside of such fills were then often integrated or hidden by painting over or onto the actual artifact surface.

Time has shown that such application of restoration materials can be detrimental to artifacts by introducing unwanted substances, obscuring manufacturing details, and covering, encasing, or otherwise obliterating other information. For instance, organic residues that may be present on the interior of a vessel but which may or may not be visible to the naked eye can retain details about the prior contents or use of the artifact. Early researchers tended to be more interested in the form of artifacts than in their contents, as food residues and the like were not easily analyzed on-site. Traces of contents or use can now be readily identified by a variety of modern

Fig. 124
Spyros Spyropoulos, the last chief pot-mender employed by the Agora excavations, is shown mending a vessel.

scientific methods. It is imperative that restoration work today does not contaminate or interfere with such research.

At the Agora, conservators still use fill materials such as plaster to support unstable original sections. Plaster and all other fills are applied judiciously, however, and separated from the artifact's surface with a barrier material that will allow the restoration to be removed if required in the future. Restored areas are then carefully painted to visually integrate yet simultaneously distinguish them from the surrounding original elements.

With old restorations currently failing or damaging artifacts, conservators are faced with re-treating large portions of archaeological collections. The challenge comes in determining what can be saved or modified and what can be removed and redone. As noted earlier, many old restorations can be seen as historical. By integrating old, nonharmful restorations, part of the artifact's treatment history is preserved. Re-treatment can also be very labor-intensive. Thus, modifying and reusing old restorations can save both time and cost.

There is now a better understanding of how storage conditions such as temperature, humidity, overcrowding, pollution, accumulation of dust, and even the choice of storage furniture itself can adversely affect finds, especially those that have undergone

Fig. 125
Storage conditions such as temperature, humidity, overcrowding, pollution, accumulation of dust, and even the choice of storage furniture itself can adversely affect finds, especially those that have undergone past chemical treatments. In this example, salts have lifted the glaze on a lamp.

past chemical treatments. Examples that have been recorded at the Agora include the growth of salt crystals in ceramics (Fig. 125) and the appearance of specific corrosion products on metal artifacts.

Finally, preventive care, arguably the most important aspect of conservation, has recently been taken one step further at the Agora. Preservation starts on-site with containers modified for humidity-sensitive artifacts, and certain long-term storage areas have been redesigned to protect specific materials, such as the metals collection. It is hoped that these measures will safely carry excavated finds through the coming decades and help preserve the collections for future scholars.

Recent Case Studies

Two finds from recent excavations, a coin hoard and a baby burial, have drawn attention as their discoveries have raised questions yet to be answered. The conservators have acted alongside the archaeologists and other specialists to meet the challenge of preserving these finds with the hope of providing some insight into the mysteries surrounding their origins.

Silver Coin Hoard

In 2005, archaeologists resumed digging the so-called Strategeion, the headquarters of the 10 generals. The area was excavated in the 1930s but recently, as discussed in Chapter 2, the building's identity had come into question and scholars were seeking information that would help reveal the structure's original use. A remarkable find was uncovered during the final weeks of the new excavations: a hoard of silver Athenian *tetradrachm* coins bearing the head and owl of Athena.

The hoard, corroded together in a lump from years of burial, was recovered in one piece by the archaeologists, apart from 47 coins that were excavated separately. Once out of the ground, the hoard was brought directly to the conservation laboratory. The lump's peculiar shape suggests that the coins were buried in some sort of sack (Fig. 126), and the conservators closely examined the soil still clinging to the hoard for clues that could indicate whether the sack was leather or textile.

Conservators weighed each of the 47 loose coins and found that although they are not similar in shape, they are remarkably similar in weight. The total weight of the lump was then divided by the average weight of the loose coins and it was estimated that the hoard consists of 400 tetradrachms. Preliminary cleaning by the conservation team to remove the burial soil was begun on five coins, which allowed the numismatist to date them to the second half of the 4th century B.C. As mentioned in Chapter 1, numismatic and metallographic studies carried out on similar coins have shown that the silver used to mint such currency probably came from the great silver mines south of Athens at Laurion.

The coins are covered with a thick, bulky, lavender-gray layer of corrosion acquired during burial, which obscures the tetradrachms' original surface. Visual examination of the coins using microscopes suggested that the corrosion is of a particular type that is best treated with a chemical method that loosens the corrosion layer and reduces the corroded silver surface back to metallic silver. As the application of chemicals is undertaken only in special circumstances, it was necessary to confirm the composition of the corrosion crust as well as the alloy content of the silver before proceeding with the treatment.

A selection of coins were chosen for micro X-ray fluorescence (μ-XRF) analysis, a technique that uses an X-ray beam to produce characteristic X-rays of the individual elements that compose the analyzed area. Scientists from the Institute of Nuclear Physics at Greece's National Center of Scientific Research «Demokritos» performed the μ-XRF analysis, the results of which indicated that the silver alloy is composed mainly of very pure silver and the corrosion layers are composed mostly of silver compounds for which the chemical reduction treatment is appropriate.

To date, around 30 coins from the hoard have been cleaned by the reduction method. The treatment so far has clarified minute details of the coins' relief motifs (Fig. 127). As the numismatist and archaeologists eagerly wait, conservators are proceeding with the treatment of the hoard to reveal the details of this exceptional find.

Fig. 126
The silver coin hoard discovered in 2005 was recovered from the ground as a single lump. Once out of the ground, the whole lump was moved to the conservation laboratory.

Byzantine Baby Burial

During the 2006 excavation season, the conservation team was summoned from the laboratory to the site to help recover a pot. Conservators were directed to a 15 cm hole in a dirt floor located in the corner of a structure. The structure was identified as either a room or courtyard of a Byzantine domestic dwelling dating to the 10th–11th century A.D. Part of what appeared to be a small skull and several bones, partially covered with soil and pottery sherds, was visible through the hole. It was clear from the start that the vessel was a Byzantine coarse ware cooking pot buried upside down and the hole was where the base of the pot had collapsed inward.

The hole and surrounding area were photographed to help record the exact location and condition of the pot and bones before they were retrieved from the trench and any surrounding evidence disturbed. Next, the floor of the room was excavated to the same depth as the exposed portion of the pot, one layer at a time, and every stage recorded. The archaeologists continued to carefully remove dirt from around the outside of the pot with small brushes, dental implements, and wooden tools until roughly a sixth of the vessel was exposed. With light shining through the cracks, the conservation team moved in to stabilize the breaks and prevent the pot from collapsing. An easily removable wax was applied along the cracks and the outside of the pot was wrapped in elastic medical bandages for further support. The work continued with the archaeologists digging away the dirt and the conservators applying wax and wrapping bandages around the freshly exposed cracks (Fig. 128).

The last part of the pot was excavated with the assistance of the anthropologist who had been called to the site to examine the bones. The team was careful to include all the remaining soil surrounding the pot when lifting the artifact out of the ground, ensuring that any bones that might have spilled out of the pot during burial, or the possible remains of a textile cover, were not disturbed until the artifact could be more closely examined in the laboratory. As a final stage in the field, the pot was cautiously lifted onto a board used as a ministretcher and carefully lowered into a basin. The artifact was supported with sandbags and the basin was immediately carried to the conservation laboratory.

Once it was in the laboratory, the conservators lifted the vessel out of the basin, allowing the earth containing the burial to gently slide from the mouth of the pot without disturbing the articulation of the bones. The anthropologist and an assistant cleared away the dirt from the bones with a set of fine brushes and small tools. Within a couple of hours they had revealed a tiny human skeleton, lying face down with its hands and legs open to the sides, knees and elbows bent close to the body (Fig. 129). The anthropologist measured the femur leg bone and determined the skeleton belonged to a fetus 32–34 weeks old.

After two months, the wax used to stabilize the cooking pot in the field had sublimated. The cracks on the inside of the vessel were again visible, and

Fig. 127
Athenian tetradrachm before and after conservation treatment. The corrosion was analyzed using X-ray fluorescence to confirm the composition of the crust as well as the alloy content of the silver before proceeding with cleaning.

Fig. 128
Stabilizing the Byzantine cooking pot in situ.

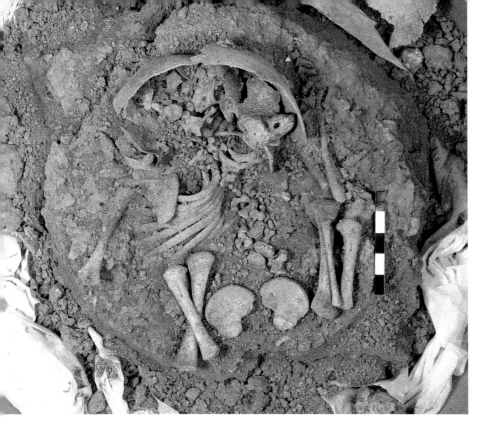

Fig. 129
Fetal skeleton, between 32 and 34 weeks old, found in
Byzantine cooking pot.

indeed extensive. The bandages were removed and cracked sections were gently deconstructed. The fragments of the pot, including the base sherds removed from the pot when it was still in the ground, were then joined together with a conservation-grade adhesive. Finally, the vessel was viewed for the first time in its entirety and the archaeologist was able to fully identify the cooking pot as a very large type B two-handled, round-bodied *tsoukali*.

Why this 10th- to 11th-century A.D. child was buried in an upside-down pot we may never know.

Severe penalties for not baptizing a baby before it dies are known from medieval canon law codes. As the burial was found under the floor of a domestic dwelling, is it possible that the baby was kept with the family and the birth never made public for fear of punishment?

Where Are We after 75 Years?

Today, the pot-menders' workspace in the Stoa of Attalos, with its microscopes and large overhanging fume extractors, looks less like an artisan's workshop and more like a scientific laboratory. The name on the door has been changed from *synkoleterion* to «Conservation Laboratory», and conservators now occupy the benches (Fig. 130).

Over time, the number of finds recovered each year has fallen, owing in part to a shorter season, fewer excavators in the field, and changes in excavation techniques. With the current approach to conservation, however, it still takes roughly 12 months to complete the work of one season.

The old pot-menders were highly skilled artisans who were self-taught and also learned their trade through apprenticeship. The new conservators spring from an academic branch, having acquired a formal university education based in the sciences and arts. But although many of the treatment methods have changed and the focus has partially shifted from the full restoration of individual artifacts to preventive and long-term care of the collection as a whole, for the most part the purpose of reconstructing pottery has remained the same for 75 years – to study, preserve, and publish the past.

Fig. 130
Today, the pot-menders' workspace in the Stoa of Attalos has been converted to a modern conservation laboratory equipped with microscopes and large overhanging fume extractors.

Anchoring the Floating Monuments of the Agora

by Richard C. Anderson

The title of this paper pays homage to my predecessor as architect to the Agora excavations, William Bell Dinsmoor Jr., who published his architectural study «Anchoring Two Floating Temples» in *Hesperia*, the journal of the American School of Classical Studies at Athens, in 1982. In that article he swapped sets of Doric and Ionic architectural pieces that had previously been assigned to two temple foundations at the Agora to achieve what is certainly a better fit in both cases. As I came to know more about the Agora, I noted the wry and perhaps ironic touch in Dinsmoor's nautical metaphor because I observed that the foundations for these temples, upon which his restorations would rest, could be seen to drift even by meters when observed on different Agora drawings. Dinsmoor, I am sure, was aware of this problem and perhaps he chose his metaphor because he knew it was applicable on another level: ships riding at anchor are not precisely fixed in one position, they are free to move and turn with the wind and tide.

The Early Surveys

This paper is about surveying at the Agora and its drawn presentation in Agora publications. It will touch upon the surveying profession, nothing short of maniacally dedicated to accuracy, and contrast it with the architectural profession that traditionally achieves its accuracy through written dimensions rather than by precise drawing. It will examine the historical consequences of abandoning the standards of both professions with regard to accuracy and it will finish with a brief description of how today's excavators are fixing these problems at the Agora. We are adjusting the shrunken or stretched mooring cables of our monuments so that they will ride on paper (or in the virtual world of the computer) where they actually ride on the site.

When the Agora excavations began in 1931, they were from their outset a grand endeavor. Land acquisition had preceded the digging by several years and, for the process of purchasing land, a great, detailed survey of the site had been undertaken. Thus, after the land had been purchased and when the digging actually began, the excavators were in possession of a remarkably trustworthy overall plan of the site. This plan, on several sheets, showed the site as it then existed, which of course meant that it showed the streets and houses that were present on the site before the beginning of the excavation (Fig. 131).

These fine-line, ink drawings on drafting linen were prepared by the surveying department of the Greek Ministry of Communications at a scale of 1:500. The individual building plots were measured and drawn by professional surveyors, as carefully and accurately as it was possible to do at that time. Accuracy was demanded by law since these survey drawings were in fact legal documents that helped to establish the fair values of the many individual properties that were to be purchased in order to allow the excavation to proceed. If the accuracy of the drawings were ever cast into doubt, there would be serious legal consequences.

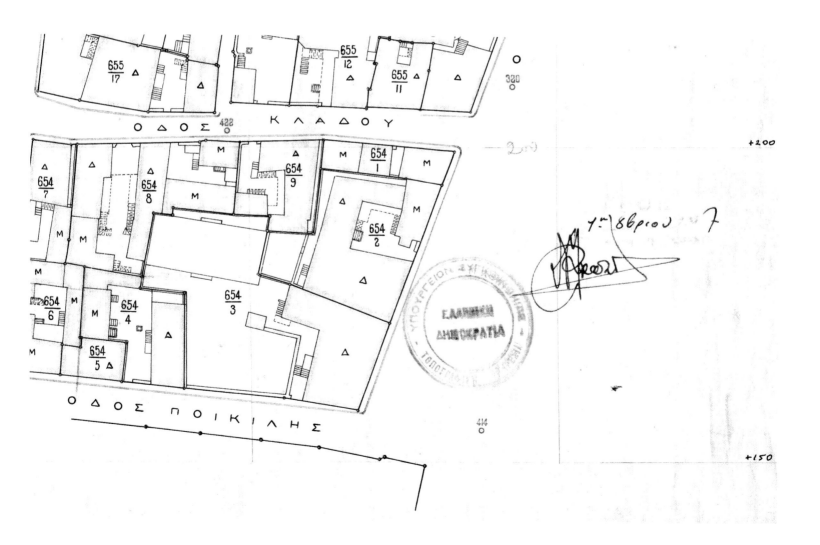

When the digging began in 1931, these survey drawings were used to provide an accurate frame of reference on which to superimpose the archaeological discoveries as they were gradually revealed. The problem that immediately arose was that the first thing the excavation necessarily did was to remove exactly what was shown on the drawings; the streets and houses that had been so carefully surveyed. The real, tangible frame of reference began to disappear.

At first, the problem could be ignored because the demolition process was carried out over several years and the first few Agora sections (areas of the excavation) were still well defined by the standing buildings that remained around their perimeters. Each new section was provided with its own section grid, innovatively defined by carefully positioned overhead wires placed at fixed intervals, and these grids were used to plan and record the archae-

ological remains within the section. These section plans, when reduced to the 1:500 scale of the expropriation survey, fitted accurately enough into the vacant spaces on the plan that were created by the erasure of the buildings that had previously been shown.

As the work proceeded over the 1930s, each subsequent area of buildings that was demolished left fewer and fewer intact streets and houses upon which the excavators could fix their new grids and thus plot their discoveries. In the post-World War II period, when the restoration of the Stoa of Attalos was completed and the last surviving block of buildings on the site, the Old Excavation House, was demolished, it was clear that the accurate frame of reference that had been provided by the original survey drawings had been lost. By then no less than 30 local section grids had been established, and none of these had ever been professionally surveyed nor

Fig. 131
Detail of a corner of one of the original, detailed survey drawings of the Agora exhibiting all the hallmarks of good, professional surveying. The drawings were legal documents and they are individually stamped and signed by the chief surveyor. True-to-scale accuracy is controlled by the 50-meter grid lines of the Athenian city grid.

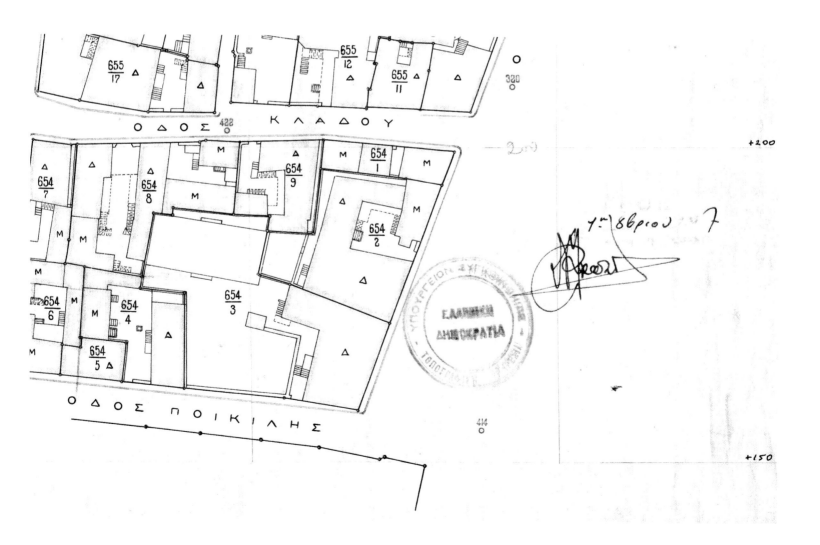

Fig. 132
A detail of Agora drawing 654, the most complete «actual state plan», at 1:500, with the same part of Agora drawing 873, a «restored plan» (of the Agora at the end of the 5th century B.C.), supposed to be at the same scale, placed over it on a light table. The two drawings are aligned in the area of the Temple of Hephaistos but can be seen to diverge by about 3 m in the area of the Altar of the Twelve Gods. This discrepancy is probably mostly due to uncontrolled expansion and contraction of fiber-based drafting materials. Without a controlling grid, the «restored plan» is not, and could never have been considered to be, an accurate, scaled drawing.

were they defined in terms of the Athenian city grid coordinates.

Significant inaccuracies began to appear in Agora drawings (Fig. 132). In addition to the loss of a working frame of reference on the site, many Agora drawings, especially those for publication, were prepared without any kind of controlling grid shown on the drawing. Intended to be simple and clear, these drawings were originally traced from the gridded, and thus true-to-scale (cartographic), source drawings but then various versions were certainly traced from each other, with each successive tracing operation introducing inaccuracy. Most published Agora drawings neither show a grid (the cartographic approach to maintaining accuracy) nor actual, denoted dimensions (the architectural method of verifying dimensional precision). Inexact tracing exacerbated by inaccuracy introduced by the expansion and contraction of fiber based drafting materials eventually meant that no dimension remained trustworthy on these drawings. It was clear that steps had to be taken to improve this situation.

Establishing a Uniform Grid

It was not until 1970 that the excavators, now led in the field by T. Leslie Shear Jr., addressed the problem of the loss of the frame of reference on the site. John Travlos, then chief architect, engaged a firm of professional surveyors, the well known Athenian firm of Ioannis Bantekas. Bantekas carried a traverse around the central area and northern perimeter of the Agora site in 1970 and established 11 bronze surveying monuments, set in concrete. In 1971, the firm carried another traverse around the eastern perimeter of the site, adding 10 monuments. Each of these 21 monuments was defined in terms of the Athenian city grid coordinates to centimetric accuracy and it is from these monuments that all of the subsequent surveying of the Agora has been carried out. This city grid had been projected over all of the emerging city of Athens in the mid-19th century and was used by archaeologists working on most of the important Athenian sites. A uniform grid allows distances to be calculated and orientations to be compared between any accurately surveyed monuments within the city.

The Bantekas traverses of 1970 and 1971 were only the first steps along the way toward re-anchoring the floating monuments. Much work was still to be done to rectify and reposition all of the earlier Agora surveying. At a minimum, two or three significant hard-edged details that were shown on the various old Agora plans and were still extant on the site could be surveyed and used first to rectify the scale, then to shift and rotate each of the old plans into its correct position. This minimal approach necessarily assumed that within the limited areas of each of the more detailed section and restored plans, there would be little internally inaccuracy.

A huge boost to this effort was provided by the highly detailed survey of the Agora site that was commissioned by the Greek Ministry of Culture as part of the plan to «unify» the archaeological sites surrounding the Acropolis in the years preceding the 2004 Olympics. Enough detail is reliably recorded on this professional «unification» survey to definitively fix almost all of the visible Agora monuments in their correct positions. With this survey, the process of eliminating inaccuracy and error from the old Agora drawings can be taken far beyond the minimal approach.

Fig. 133

An example of a 1990s Agora true-to-scale architectural field sheet, where the scale drawing has been executed in the field. Note that rubble is carefully depicted; annotated numbers refer to levels that are recorded in tables in the architect's notes. Grid lines are the global, Athenian grid.

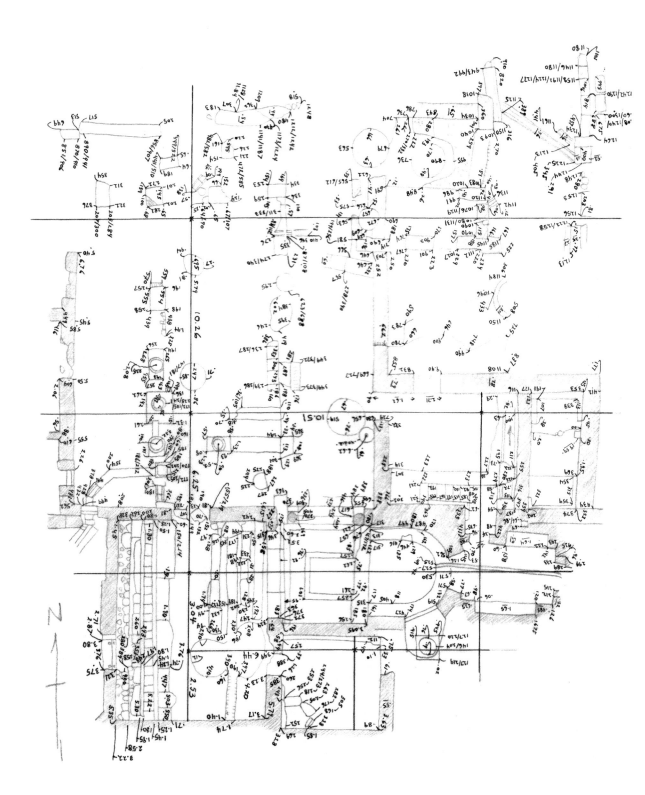

Fig. 134
A sample of field architectural recording done by William Bell Dinsmoor Jr., showing a carefully sketched freehand plan annotated with many measurements that made it possible subsequently to construct a reasonably accurate, scaled version of the drawing. Accurate, stone-by-stone depiction of non-monumental detail such as rubble walling is difficult or impossible employing this system, and any information about levels is absent.

Recent Developments

Two other changes have improved the accuracy of surveying at the Agora in recent years. The first is a simple, practical expedient: all recent drawings have been done on polyester drafting film rather than on any fiber based drafting materials. Polyester film is dimensionally highly stable, expanding or contracting about 50 times less than paper when subjected to changes in temperature and humidity.

It is also considered to be of a higher archival quality than most papers especially being immune to water and insect damage. Had this material been available long ago, far less inaccuracy would have crept into the gridded and, particularly, the ungridded Agora drawings.

The second change introduced was in the method of surveying in the field. The difference between an archaeological survey drawing and any other kind of surveying, done by even the most skilled and professional of surveyors, is that for archaeological surveying, the actual true-to-scale drawing must be executed in the field while you are looking at what you are drawing. Surveyors traditionally draw free-hand sketches in their field notebooks, which are then richly annotated with measured dimensions that give enough information for the final scale drawing to be constructed in the office. Direct, true-to-scale drawing in the field is superior to this classic surveying approach because errors and omissions can immediately be observed and much more accurate sketched detail can be added. Nor does archaeological surveying readily turn to stylized, cartographic conventions for what it depicts; trustworthy «stone-by-stone» detail is essential to make field recording as objective as possible. As an example, a recent sheet, prepared in the field (Fig. 133), can be contrasted with an older «dimensioned sketch» example, where the scale drawing was prepared later, in the office (Fig. 134). Although the latter is of excellent quality, it can be observed that the plan compiled using this old methodology must necessarily resort to «conventionalized» rubble because practically no information about rubble wall detail is included in the sketch.

Surveying in the Digital Age

The two changes described above are insignificant compared to the transition to an unquestionably modern and high-tech approach to archaeological surveying. The surveying system now in use at the Agora is one that was pioneered by Nigel R. Fradgley of English Heritage and developed for surveying historic buildings. This system began to be introduced at the Agora in 2001 and was fully up and running in the summer of 2002.

The Fradgley system is based on the use of a very fast «total station». This is an optical instrument incorporating a theodolite to measure horizontal and vertical angles and an electronic distance measure. The total station is linked to a small, field computer that runs a powerful CAD (formerly CADD, Computer-Aided Design and Drafting) system. The total station is capable of «shooting» points quickly enough to essentially «draw» objects by defining them in terms of a sequence of points sufficiently numerous to accurately record the forms of the objects. Three-dimensional coordinates of the «shot» points are transmitted from the total station to the field computer and stored directly as a «drawing» in CAD. The Fradgley software places a tiny dot at each surveyed point and connects the dots successively with lines to form three-dimensional drawings of whatever is being surveyed. Thus, three-dimensional surveyed data are expressed immediately as points and lines to form simply a faithful drawing of whatever is being surveyed rather than a more schematic drawing with fewer points and a lot of unnecessary clutter such as cartographic symbols, «feature codes», and sequential numbers, which are typically introduced by other surveying programs. A drawing is created that can be viewed in the field and verified to be an accurate rendering of whatever is being drawn.

The equipment currently in use at the Agora comprises a Leica TCR305 total station and Micro-Station CAD software running on a Fujitsu 3500S tablet computer (with an outdoor-viewable screen). The MicroStation CAD system was selected by Nigel Fradgley for his surveying system years ago because it was (and probably still is) superior for three dimensional work. More powerful and faster theodolites and computers now exist that would perhaps improve our system but a virtue of this system is that it is quite simple and not horribly expensive.

Field recording of the architectural remains at the Agora is thus now done in three dimensions, and the raw field data are expressed as «wireframe» models of whatever is surveyed, as shown in Figure 135. The actual practice in the field involves defining or «drawing» objects with a series of «shot» points that are connected in sequence by straight lines automatically generated by the Fradgley system. Layers, colors, line weights and styles, circles, and other curves (in fact, the vast panoply of CAD tools) are available in the field, although in practice it is more economical to use field time and computer battery power to draw things as completely and objectively as possible using a small repertoire of the simpler tools. This computer-aided system offers huge advantages over manual survey since thousands of points are economically «shot» to very precisely define, rather than sketch or conventionalize, detail.

Two people are normally required to operate the system, one to «shoot» with the total station and operate the computer, the second to sequentially define and mark (with a small but easy-to-see reflective target) the points that are to be recorded. Although manual drawing skills are not required, it is essential for the person defining the points to know what points should be defined, and these are essentially the points along edges that would generate lines in a conventional drawing. With all points recorded in three dimensions, the result is far more than «just» one drawing: all of the recorded information can contribute toward any kind of view. Plans at any scale, sections, and elevations can be prepared; also three-dimensional views, especially perspectives, that are extremely useful and effective for interpretation and presentation of archaeological material. The accuracy, again, is simply astonishing, reducing a few centimeters (or, in earlier times, meters) of inaccuracy in the days of hand drawing to a few millimeters today.

Computerized surveying at the Agora is safely anchoring our monuments in a new and three-

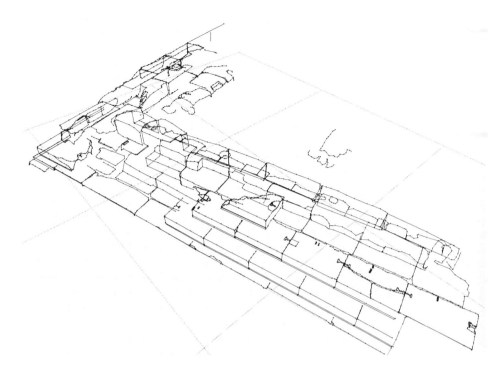

Fig. 135
An example of recent architectural field recording (showing part of the western end of the probable Painted Stoa) using the computer-enabled Fradgley system. Shown is an oblique perspective view of part of a three-dimensional wireframe model. The three-dimensionality of the drawing of such a «hard-edged» and monumental architectural subject is clear, though it would not be so for static views of less intelligible architecture. Three-dimensionality is dramatically revealed when any wireframe model is rotated on the computer screen, but it disappears immediately when the motion ceases. Clicking on any of the surveyed points (the heavier dots on the screen) will reveal the x, y, and z coordinates (plan position and level) of that point on the site grid.

dimensional sea. Anchored, each monument rides at its own level, revealing its internal chronology and relationships with its neighbors like never before. It is certain that three-dimensional surveying in CAD will become the standard method for spatially recording archaeology in the not too distant future. Now that it has been used at the Agora over a number of years, with staff learning new tricks and acquiring new skills along the way, the thought of a return to any older surveying methods becomes as unthinkable as renouncing electric light.

Applying New Technologies

by Bruce Hartzler

This is the story of a funerary stele (an ancient gravestone) identified in the Agora records as S 3497 (Fig. 136). What remains of the stele is just a single fragment from the top of what would have been a larger grave monument. The fragment depicts the head of a young woman with her right hand raised to her face, her fingers lightly resting on her cheek. She has full pouty lips and deep-set eyes. She is probably not the deceased (the deceased do not mourn for themselves). It is more likely that she is a witness in a funeral scene, perhaps a family member mourning her lost loved one.

The funerary stele was probably sculpted in the late 4th century B.C. How long it stood above the grave is unknown, but at some point it fell and broke since the fragment was found built into a much later Byzantine wall of the 10th or 11th century A.D. The fragment is square and relatively smooth on the back (a useful shape for stacking in a wall made up of rubble and dirt). It was upended more than a thousand years ago and remained that way until the summer of 2001 when, dismantling the Byzantine wall during annual excavations, the excavators turned over a flat worked stone, literally brushed the dirt from the young woman's face, and brought her back into the world.

Fig. 136
Fragment of a funerary stele (S 3497) showing a young woman, probably from the late 4th century B.C. The fragment, recovered during excavations in 2001, had been built into a much later Byzantine wall.

Recording in the Field

The Agora is fortunate in having what one might call a «second-generation» recordkeeping system. The other great sites of the Mediterranean (Troy, the Roman Forum, Delphi, Olympia, Pompeii, Knossos) all came under excavation from as early as the 18th century, at a time when detailed records of stratigraphy were not kept. Because the Agora excavations began a generation or more later, all the objects are catalogued in a single, detailed, unified recordkeeping system. Most sites excavated today are of course properly recorded, but they cannot match the Agora material in either scale or chronological range.

Lucy Talcott is credited with having developed the Agora recordkeeping system in the early 1930s. Judging from her elegant solutions for organizing archaeological data, one might say that she thought like a computer. The system designed had the advantage of being created in a time when researchers had started to realize the limitations of the recordkeeping systems from the other excavations; they were asking questions that could not be answered from the information that was being recorded. The Agora system was designed to record data in a way that could answer these new kinds of questions.

The process of excavation, recording, and research is a dynamic one and continues to evolve at the Agora today. As we move into the digital age, new questions are being asked that stretch to its limits the efficiency of the original paper-based recordkeeping system. As these new questions put pressure on how information is recorded, we have started turning to technology (and specifically computers) as a means of modernizing 75 years of archaeological data as well as the excavation process itself. If Lucy Talcott's system represents the second generation, one might say that we are now entering the third.

When the stele fragment described earlier was found and lifted from the wall, work in the immediate area paused as the buzz of a new significant find spread among the trenches. People gathered around to see the new artifact. Almost immediately, the supervisor responsible for this area began the process of cataloging the new find: the block was taken down from the wall and, as the caked dirt was gently brushed away from the young woman's face, the first photographs were taken and the call went out to «take a point».

Until very recently, a grid system was used in the Agora to describe the original findspot of an artifact (numbers like «J/1,2–4/17,18» were used to identify a specific one-meter square within the Agora site). Today, as described in Chapter 10, we use electronic theodolite systems and Palm Pilots to record points in three-dimensional space with millimeter accuracy (Fig. 137). So when the call goes out to «take a point», a rod is placed in the center of the depression where the stele fragment lay on the wall, and a theodolite returns the value (390.245, 385.977, 54.307), a precise x,y,z point on the Greek national grid. Simply by increasing the resolution of our recording, searches such as «find every sculpture fragment within 20 centimeters of a bronze coin» become possible.

Fig. 137

Archaeological data are now collected and organized on handheld Palm Pilot computers. Four screen shots show data entered in the field by the supervisor.

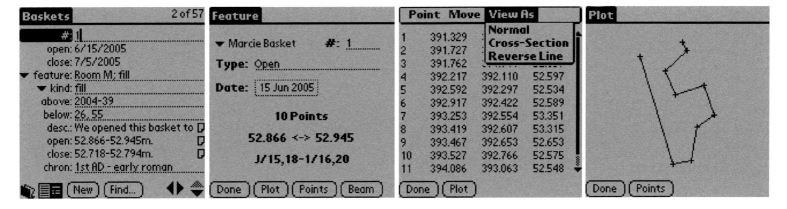

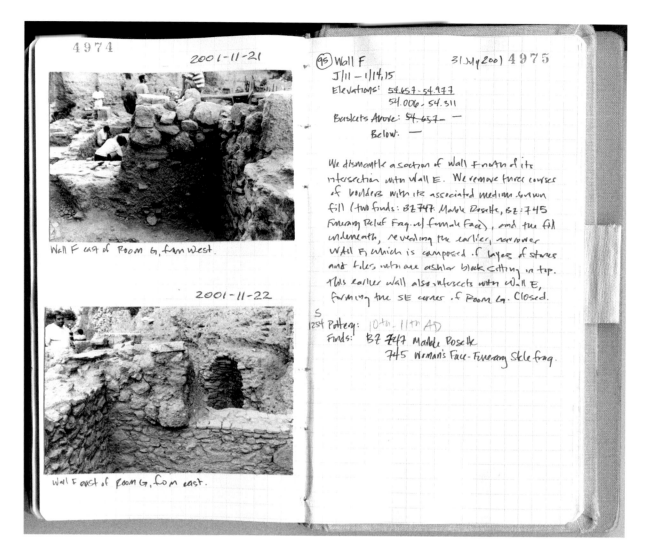

Within her field excavation notebook, the super-visor keeps a daily diary detailing the excavation of wall F from which the stele comes (Fig. 138).

We dismantled a section of Wall F north of its intersection with Wall E. We removed three courses of boulders with the associated medium-brown fill, and the fill underneath, revealing an earlier, narrower Wall F, which is composed of layers of stones and tiles with one ashlar block sitting on top. This earlier wall also intersects with Wall E, forming the south-east corner of Room G.

As she excavates, she documents her progress with narrative as well as with photographs. These days, digital cameras have replaced traditional film-based photography, removing previous constraints on the quantity of images taken in the field – the space available in a paper notebook for photography is relatively small, whereas any number of digital images can be attached to an electronic excavation narrative. In this situation, images are taken every few minutes as the dirt is brushed away from our stele and more and more of the young woman's face is revealed.

The supervisor uses a separate notebook, the finds notebook, to record detailed information on the new stele fragment (Fig. 139):

Marble Sculpture – Face
J/11–1/14
Wall F north of Wall E
BZ MID XXV p. 4975
31 July 2001
elev. 54.307
P.H. = 0.340 m
P.W. = 0.275 m
Th. = (max) 0.115 m

Top edge and front and back surfaces preserved. Fragment of a funerary stele, with the frontal face of a woman with her right hand on her cheek — four fingers preserved. Right side of hair, head broken off. Fragment of thick drapery on her left shoulder. Ear-length hair. Possibly late 4th century. Marble. Back surface roughly finished.

By cross-referencing the stele fragment from the finds notebook to a page in the excavation notebook (BZ MID XXV p. 4975), the archaeologist has effectively linked the find to its archaeological context. All the pottery sherds and other objects found during the excavation of wall F will be simi-larly cross-referenced and kept together for use in helping to discover a date for the construction of this particular wall.

These notebooks are durable bound paper note-books. For each section being excavated, there are notebooks for daily diaries, for finds, for coins, and for recording pottery lots (a pottery lot is the set of broken pottery sherds that come from a single archaeological context). The Agora has more than 850 such notebooks representing excavations from 1931 to the present. Even though the team contin-ues to use the same style of notebooks today, their significance in the field has lessened somewhat.

Fig. 139

The find notebook entry for S 3497. Detailed information on important artifacts is recorded in this notebook, which is cross-referenced to the field excavation notebook shown in Figure 138.

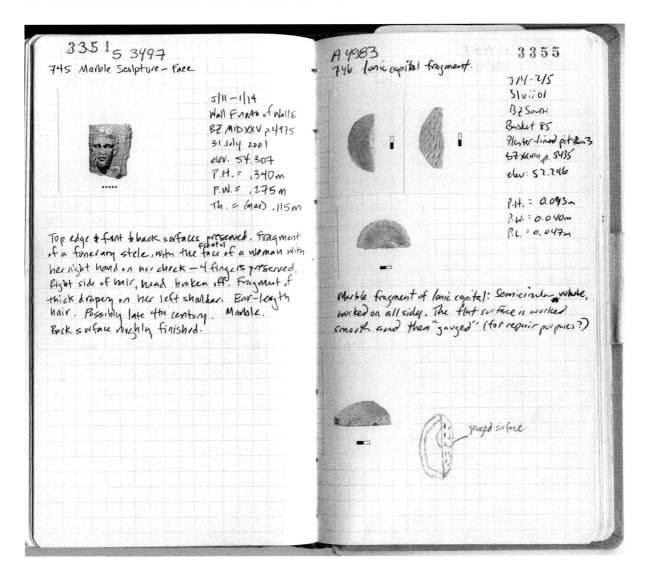

Today they are used primarily to maintain consistency with 75 years of archaeological data. The real work of writing and recording data in the field is now being done in databases on handheld computers.

So, in fact, the archaeologist has not been writing in a paper notebook at all, but on the small Palm Pilot (see Fig. 137), which she then hands to her assistant to copy the relevant information into the traditional notebooks. Where before one needed to make cross-references explicit, now databases make such links automatically. Today our archaeological record is essentially «born digital» and «backed up» onto paper.

A New Approach

In 1999, at the instigation of and with the support of the Packard Humanities Institute, the Athenian Agora began the process of digitizing our 75 years of archaeological history. This entailed creating digital versions of all our material records, whether field excavation notebooks, catalog cards for finds, photographs of excavations in progress, or architectural drawings. (This digitization process continues today with the support of the European Union and Delmas Foundation.) At the same time, we also began

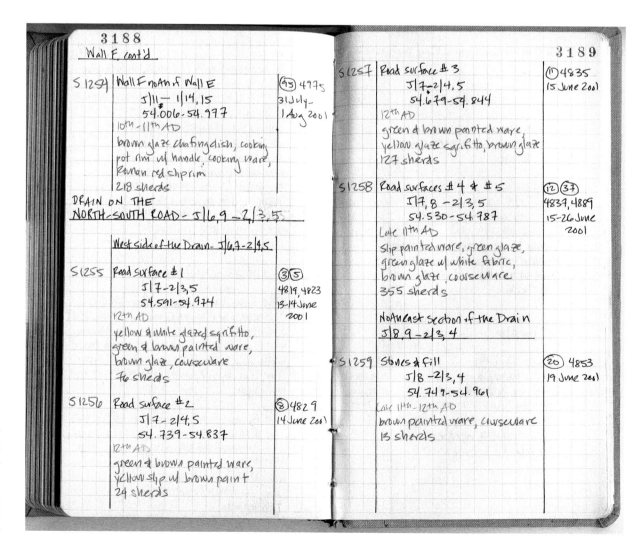

Fig. 140
The pottery notebook entry for wall F (S 1254 at the top of p. 3188) suggests a date belonging to the 10th or 11th century A.D.

the process of designing a new system for recording data in the field as we excavate.

One of the primary difficulties we faced was designing a system that would both manage the quantity of our existing materials and be flexible enough for capturing and organizing new archaeological data. We needed a system that would encapsulate the existing records about our material as well as the process of excavation and research. Essentially, we needed a system that modeled the historical nature of archaeological study and analysis itself.

Our long-term goal with this project has been the creation of a single integrated and coherent digital archive of all the archaeological resources at the Athenian Agora: from object databases, photographs, site guides, virtual-reality tours, and architectural plans and drawings to new excavation data, reports, and publications. This digital archive is searchable and accessible from anywhere by means of the Internet, freely available to higher educational institutions, students of the classical world, and communities of classical enthusiasts everywhere.

After the initial recording in the field, stele fragment S 3497 is carefully transported into the conservation laboratory, where it is processed and cleaned.

We record what conservation is carried out on the object. The resilience of marble makes it rather easy to conserve – this fragment requires just a simple bath and light scrub. The conservation database report reads as follows: «S 3497. Surface soil. Root marks. Brown patina which is not loose dirt. Surface fairly coherent but somewhat saccharoidal. No longer original polished surface. Treatment: Washed in water with a brush».

Once excavation outside on wall F has been completed, all the pottery sherds collected from the wall are washed and laid out on a table where they can be «read» and analyzed by the supervisor and director of the excavations to calculate the date of the context and hence a date for the construction of wall F. In this case, the pottery suggests a date in the 10th or 11th century A.D. This information is recorded in a pottery notebook and tracked in a database containing information on all features in the Agora (Fig. 140). It is here that the beginnings of a human-generated hierarchy forms in terms of dividing the excavated area into layers, deposits, rooms, and buildings: in this case, our stele fragment is labeled as coming from within wall F, which in turn is part of a Byzantine building east of a north–south road.

The Digital Archive

The last step for the funerary stele occurs in the records office of the Stoa of Attalos, where an official catalog card is created for the object (Fig. 141). This is the backbone of Lucy Talcott's system: one card for each of our roughly 120,000 inventoried finds. Today this essential information is also entered into an object database that serves as the backbone for our digital archive. Where before one needed to visit the Agora in person and search through drawers of cards looking for objects potentially relevant to a research topic, today one can simply visit our Web site (http://www.agathe.gr) from anywhere in the world and search or browse directly.

The inherently cross-referenced nature of archaeological material is well suited for a hypertext-based

Web interface. A user can enter our digital archive at any point (whether searching for an object, a photograph, a feature, etc.) and all related and associated records are automatically gathered and presented to the user in an integrated fashion. For example, if the stele is selected, the user is presented with inventory information for this object, publication records and commentary, associated photographs (from in situ to final publication), its conservation history, any drawings made of the object, plans showing the location where this object was found, movies of this object if they exist (either being excavated or QTVR – QuickTime virtual reality – object movies), links to various typologies to which the object may belong, references to the original excavation context, and narrative of when this object was first uncov-

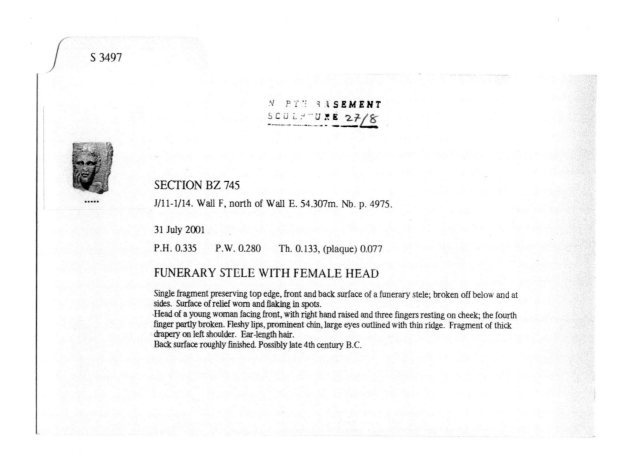

S 3497

N PTH BASEMENT
SCULPTURE 27/8

SECTION BZ 745

J/11-1/14. Wall F, north of Wall E. 54.307m. Nb. p. 4975.

31 July 2001

P.H. 0.335   P.W. 0.280   Th. 0.133, (plaque) 0.077

FUNERARY STELE WITH FEMALE HEAD

Single fragment preserving top edge, front and back surface of a funerary stele; broken off below and at sides. Surface of relief worn and flaking in spots.
Head of a young woman facing front, with right hand raised and three fingers resting on cheek; the fourth finger partly broken. Fleshy lips, prominent chin, large eyes outlined with thin ridge. Fragment of thick drapery on left shoulder. Ear-length hair.
Back surface roughly finished. Possibly late 4th century B.C.

Fig. 141
The catalog card for S 3497. An official catalogue card is created for each inventoried object, now amounting to more than 160,000 finds.

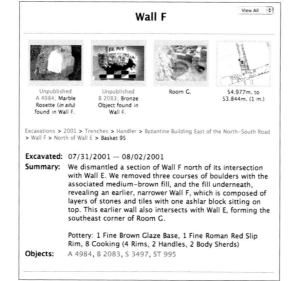

Wall F   View All

Unpublished   Unpublished   Room G.   54.977m. to
A 4984: Marble   B 2083: Bronze   53.844m. (1 m.)
Rosette (in situ) Object found in
found in Wall F. Wall F.

Excavations > 2001 > Trenches > Handler > Byzantine Building East of the North-South Road > Wall F > North of Wall E > Basket 95

Excavated: 07/31/2001 — 08/02/2001
Summary: We dismantled a section of Wall F north of its intersection with Wall E. We removed three courses of boulders with the associated medium-brown fill, and the fill underneath, revealing an earlier, narrower Wall F, which is composed of layers of stones and tiles with one ashlar block sitting on top. This earlier wall also intersects with Wall E, forming the southeast corner of Room G.

            Pottery: 1 Fine Brown Glaze Base, 1 Fine Roman Red Slip Rim, 8 Cooking (4 Rims, 2 Handles, 2 Body Sherds)
Objects: A 4984, B 2083, S 3497, ST 995

S 3497   View All

Excavations > BZ North > Features > Building East of the North-South Road > Walls > Wall F > North of Wall E > Basket 95

Catalog Entry

Inventory #: S 3497
Title: Funerary Stele with Female Head
Section #:   BZ 745
Category: Sculpture
Basket: 95
Entry Date: 31 July 2001
Description: Single fragment preserving top edge, front and back surface of a funerary stele; broken off below and at sides. Surface of relief worn and flaking in spots.

              Head of a young woman facing front, with right hand raised and three fingers resting on cheek; the fourth finger partly broken. Fleshy lips, prominent chin, large eyes outlined with thin ridge. Fragment of thick drapery on left shoulder. Ear-length hair.

              Back surface roughly finished. Possibly late 4th century B.C.
Context: Wall F, north of Wall E.
Dimensions: P.H. 0.335; P.W. 0.280; Th. 0.133, (plaque) 0.077
Levels: 54.307m.
Material: Marble
NB Pages: 4975
Negatives: no photo
New Grid: J/11-1/14
Storage: North Basement-Sculpture, Block 27/8

54.307m. to 54.006m. (2 cm.)

S 3497: Marble Face found in Wall F.

S 3497: Marble Face found in Wall F.

Fig. 142
Screen-captures showing the feature «Wall F» and the object «S 3497».

ered. Similar types of links are automatically generated when a user selects an image, feature, plan, or movie (Fig. 142).

A digital archive has several immediate advantages over traditional paper-based records. The most obvious is the ease with which you can search and collect information that may have been recorded over several years of field excavations. Where before you were required to sift through pages and pages of notebooks, now you can gather the relevant in-

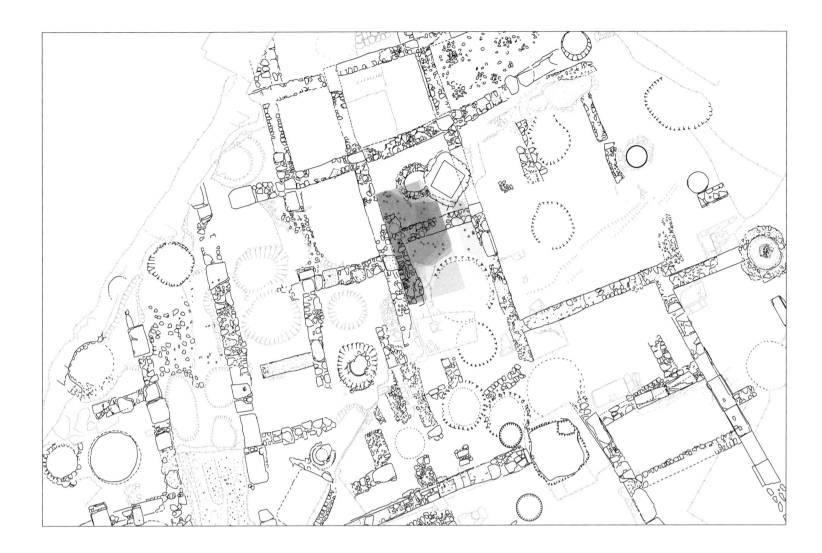

formation almost instantly (and from anywhere). Since the digital discovery and presentation process is dynamic, the archive essentially evolves as more information is added. Having data «born digitally» in the field is also advantageous. Field data can be immediately synthesized (with previous seasons) or rearranged (hierarchically, chronologically, typologically, etc.) and then returned to the excavators during the same excavation season, to be used as an additional resource for guiding the excavation process itself.

Several interfaces for the digital archive have been developed. At the most basic level, a keyword search searches all data sources simultaneously. Another interface is through the use of human-generated topographical and thematic hierarchies. The spine of the topographical hierarchy is the Agora's published site guide, dividing it into major areas, build-

ings, and features (the Temple of Hephaistos, the Panathenaic Way, the Crossroads Enclosure, etc.). Objects and photographs can then be located within this browsable hierarchy, generating typologies such as «Architecture and Topography > Temple of Hephaistos > Sculpture > West Pediment».

The benefit of using such hierarchies is that one can group and retrieve items at any level. For example, one might begin with a typology that points to a precise unit of excavation: «Section BZ > Byzantine Building > Room G > Wall F» and then from here it is easy to ascend and collect all finds, features, photographs, and commentary located at the «Room G» level, the «Byzantine Building» level, or even the entire «Section BZ» level. This collation or grouping closely resembles a predominant type of research performed on the material. And where such grouping in the past was often a time-

Fig. 143
A plan of the Byzantine building with a dynamic distribution map overlay.

consuming and tedious enterprise with traditional paper notebooks and catalog cards, a computer can accomplish the same task quickly and efficiently.

Another benefit of digital archaeological data is that field data can be easily integrated into maps and drawings or exported into traditional GIS (geographical information systems) based applications. Questions can now be asked (and answered) that were not possible before simply because of the difficulty of collecting all relevant data. For example, it is possible to generate distribution maps for objects based on time, place, type, or any other qualifier, and then display the results of such a query on user-selected plans, all in real time. Or to do the reverse, one can select an area from a plan and generate a list of all objects found within that area. We can even create time-based simulations (movies) to track the distribution of objects over a period of years or even centuries (Fig. 143).

As mentioned earlier, one of the primary difficulties the Agora excavation project faced in the development of its digital archive was designing a system that encapsulated the historical nature of archaeological study itself. Since archaeological data can at any moment be reevaluated, reorganized, redated, and reinterpreted, ideally one wants to preserve this history of analysis in addition to the most current and authoritative view. There does not have to be a «final word» with respect to digital archaeological data, only an ongoing open-ended analysis — a versioned history, so to speak — where one can see how a building, room, or object was interpreted and understood at any point in its history.

Once we view archaeological data in this way (from a historical or versioned point of view), nearly all difficulties in modeling complex archaeological data are eliminated. Objects that are split or joined with other objects simply carry their history with them. When terminology changes over time, objects remember their many different names. When an object is reclassified or republished or redated, it remembers when, by whom, where, and why. All

these actions simply become moments in an object's history. Thus the digital archive models the excavation process itself, from the initial discovery and guesswork to researched theories and conclusions. There is no need to replace the paper records that represent 75 years of excavation at the Agora; we have simply included them as significant moments in the lives of our archaeological artifacts.

Soon after the funerary stele S 3497 was discovered, recorded, and brought into the Agora system, when the curious archaeologists had all returned to their trenches, work continued on wall F until a short time later, when a bright white marble edge appeared in the courses of the wall: a fragment of a marble rosette (Fig. 144). Wall F, it seemed, had not finished revealing its secrets, and the process we have witnessed here was about to repeat itself all over again: A 4984 had been found.

⇦⤢ Fig. 144

A marble rosette (A 4984) found in wall F, shown in situ (left) and in detail (above).

CHRONOLOGY AND FURTHER READING

Chronology

ca. 3000 B.C.	Earliest recorded habitation in Athens on the Acropolis slopes
1550–1100 B.C.	Mycenaean Period (Late Helladic or Late Bronze Age)
1100–700 B.C.	Protogeometric and Geometric periods
700–480 B.C.	Archaic period
ca. 600 B.C.	First democratic city government, under Solon (594 B.C.)
566–510 B.C.	Rule of Peisistratos and his sons
566 B.C.	The Panathenaia, festival in honor of Athena, founded (or reorganized) on a grand scale
514 B.C.	Tyrant Hipparchos killed by Harmodios and Aristogeiton
508/7 B.C.	Democratic reforms under Kleisthenes
490–479 B.C.	The Persian Wars (sack of Athens by the Persians, 480/79 B.C.)
480–323 B.C.	Classical period
460–429 B.C.	Age of Perikles
431–404 B.C.	Peloponnesian War (Peace of Nikias, 421–415 B.C.)
399 B.C.	Death of Sokrates
362 B.C.	Battle of Mantineia
338 B.C.	Supremacy of Macedon (Battle of Chaironeia); Lykourgos in charge of Athenian finances, 338–326 B.C.
323 B.C.	Death of Alexander the Great
323–146 B.C.	Hellenistic period
322 B.C.	Macedonian occupation of Athens
159–138 B.C.	Attalos II King of Pergamon (Stoa of Attalos constructed ca. 150 B.C.)
146 B.C.	Ascendancy of Rome (sack of Corinth by Mummius)
146 B.C.– A.D. 337	Roman period
86 B.C.	Siege of Athens by Sulla
27 B.C.– A.D. 14	Reign of Augustus
A.D. 117–138	Reign of Hadrian
A.D. 138–161	Reign of Antoninus Pius (visit of Pausanias to Athens ca. A.D. 150)
A.D. 267	Buildings in the Agora burned by the Herulians
A.D. 337–700	Late Roman or Byzantine period
A.D. 396	Invasion by Visigoths under Alaric
A.D. 467	Possible attack on Athens by Vandals
A.D. 529	Schools of Athens closed by the Emperor Justinian
A.D. 582/3	Devastation probably caused by Slavs
A.D. 1204	Lower city of Athens devastated by Leon Sgouros from Nauplia
A.D. 1456–1458	Capture of Athens by the Turks (lower city, A.D. 1457; Acropolis, A.D. 1458)
A.D. 1821–1828	Greek War of Independence
A.D. 1834	Athens becomes the capital of modern Greece
A.D. 1881	American School of Classical Studies at Athens established
A.D. 1931	American excavations in the Agora begin
A.D. 1956	Reconstructed Stoa of Attalos dedicated as Agora research center
A.D. 2006	75th anniversary of the beginning of American excavations in the Athenian Agora

FURTHER READING

The Archaeology of the Agora: A Summary

Many of the topics reviewed here have been the subject of individual accounts in the Agora Picture Books series, some 25 of which have been published by the American School of Classical Studies at Athens (available from http://www.ascsa.edu.gr/publications and from http://www.agathe.gr).

For more general accounts, see:

Agora III = R. E. Wycherley, *Literary and Epigraphical Testimonia* (1957).

Agora XIV = H. A. Thompson / R. E. Wycherley, *The Agora of Athens: The History, Shape, and Uses of an Ancient City Center* (1972).

F. Börner, *Die bauliche Entwicklung Athens als Handelsplatz in archaischer und klassischer Zeit* (1996).

J. McK. Camp II, *The Athenian Agora* (1992).

J. McK. Camp II, *Die Agora von Athen: Ausgrabungen im Herzen des klassischen Athen* (1994).

J. McK. Camp II, *The Athenian Agora: Site Guide* (2010).

Recent discoveries in the Agora are summarized in *Hesperia: The Journal of the American School of Classical Studies at Athens.*

J. McK. Camp II, Excavations in the Athenian Agora, 1996 and 1997, in: *Hesperia* 68 (1999) 268–274.

J. McK. Camp II, Excavations in the Athenian Agora, 2002–2007, in: *Hesperia* 76 (2006) 627–663.

Commerce and Crafts around the Athenian Agora

Agora III = R. E. Wycherley, *Literary and Epigraphical Testimonia* (1957) 149–150, 174–177, 185–206.

Agora XIV = H. A. Thompson / R. E. Wycherley, *The Agora of Athens: The History, Shape, and Uses of an Ancient City Center* (1972) 170–173, 185–191.

M. Bettalli, Case, botteghe, *ergasteria*: Note sui luoghi di produzione e di vendita nell'Atene classica, in: *Opus* 4 (1985) 29–42.

M. L. Lawall, Graffiti, Wine Selling, and the Reuse of Amphoras in the Athenian Agora, ca. 430–400 B.C., in: *Hesperia* 69 (2000) 3–90.

T. L. Milbank, *A Commercial and Industrial Building in the Athenian Agora, 480 B.C. to A.D. 125* (2002).

D. B. Thompson, *An Ancient Shopping Center: The Athenian Agora, Agora Picture Book* 12 (1971).

E. Vanderpool, The State Prison of Ancient Athens, in: K. DeVries (ed.), *From Athens to Gordion: The Papers of a Memorial Symposium for Rodney S. Young* (1980) 17–31.

R. S. Young, An Industrial District of Ancient Athens, in: *Hesperia* 20 (1951) 135–288.

Living Near the Agora: Houses and Households in Central Athens

Agora XIV = H. A. Thompson / R. E. Wycherley, *The Agora of Athens: The History, Shape, and Uses of an Ancient City Center* (1972) 178–185.

N. D. Cahill, *Household and City Organization at Olynthus* (2002).

J. McK. Camp II, *Die Agora von Athen: Ausgrabungen im Herzen des klassischen Athen* (1994) 169–171; *The Athenian Agora* (1992) 140–142.

M. Goldberg, Spatial and Behavioral Negotiation in Classical Athenian City Houses, in: P. Allison (ed.), *Household Archaeology* (1999) 142–161.

J. W. Graham, Houses of Classical Athens, in: *Phoenix* 28 (1974) 45–54.

W. Hoepfner (ed.), *Geschichte des Wohnens 1. 5000 B.C.–500 A.D.: Vorgeschichte, Frühgeschichte, Antike* (1999).

L. C. Nevett, *House and Society in the Ancient Greek World* (1999).

D. B. Thompson, The House of Simon the Shoemaker, in: *Archaeology* 13 (1960) 234–240.

G. Thür, Wo wohnen die Metöken? in: W. Schuller / W. Hoepfner / E. L. Schwandner (eds.), *Demokratie und Architektur: Der hippodamische Städtebau und die Entstehung der Demokratie* (1989) 117–121.

B. Tsakirgis, Living and Working around the Athenian Agora. A Preliminary Case Study of Three Houses, in: B. A. Ault / L. C. Nevett (eds.), *Ancient Greek Houses and Households: Chronological, Regional, and Social Diversity* (2005) 67–82.

S. Walker, Women and Housing in Classical Greece. The Archaeological Evidence, in: A. Cameron / A. Kuhrt (eds.), *Images of Women in Antiquity* (1983) 81–91.

R. S. Young, An Industrial District of Ancient Athens, in: *Hesperia* 20 (1951) 135–288.

Roman Portraits from the Athenian Agora: Recent Finds

Agora I = E. B. Harrison, *Portrait Sculpture* (1953).

E. B. Harrison, *Ancient Portraits from the Athenian Agora, Agora Picture Book* 5 (1960).

E. B. Harrison, New Sculpture from the Athenian Agora, in: *Hesperia* 29 (1960) 369–392.

L. A. Riccardi, The Bust-Crown, the Panhellenion, and Eleusis: A New Portrait from the Athenian Agora, in: *Hesperia* 76 (2007) 365–390.

The Wine Jars Workroom: Stamps to Sherds

V. R. Grace, Stamped Amphora Handles Found in 1931–1932, in: *Hesperia* 3 (1934) 197–310.

V. R. Grace, The Eponyms Named on Rhodian Amphora Stamps, in: *Hesperia* 22 (1953) 116–128.

V. R. Grace, *Amphoras and the Ancient Wine Trade, Agora Picture Book* 6 (1979 rev. ed.).

V. R. Grace, Notes on Amphoras from the Koroni Peninsula, in: *Hesperia* 32 (1963) 319–334.

V. R. Grace, Samian Amphoras, in: *Hesperia* 40 (1971) 52–95.

V. R. Grace, The Middle Stoa Dated by Amphora Stamps, in: *Hesperia* 54 (1985) 1–54.

V. R. Grace / M. Savvatianou-Petropoulakou, Les timbres amphoriques grecs, in: *Exploration archéologique de Délos 27: L'ilot de la Maison des Comédiens* (1970) 277–382.

C. G. Koehler, Virginia Randolph Grace, 1901–1994, in: *American Journal of Archaeology* 100 (1996) 153–155.

S. I. Rotroff / R. D. Lamberton, *Women in the Athenian Agora, Agora Picture Book* 26 (2005) 50.

The Persian Destruction Deposits and the Development of Pottery Research at the Agora Excavations

For an ancient account of the Persian Wars, see Herodotus, *The Persian Wars*. Modern bibliography relevant to the Persian destruction deposits is:

Agora XII = B. A. Sparkes / L. Talcott, *Black and Plain Pottery of the 6th, 5th, and 4th Centuries B.C.* (1970).

E. Francis / M. Vickers, The Agora Revisited: Athenian Chronology c. 500–450 B.C., in: *Papers of the British School at Athens* 83 (1988) 143–167.

B. Graef / E. Langlotz, *Die antiken Vasen von der Akropolis zu Athen* (1909–1933).

M. L. Lawall, Graffiti, Wine Selling, and the Reuse of Amphoras in the Athenian Agora, ca. 430–400 B.C., in: *Hesperia* 69 (2000) 3–90.

K. Lynch, *The Symposium in Context: Pottery from a Late Archaic Athenian House, Hesperia* Suppl. (in prep.).

S. Roberts, The Stoa Gutter Well, a Late Archaic Deposit in the Athenian Agora, in: *Hesperia* 55 (1986) 1–74.

S. I. Rotroff / J. H. Oakley, *Debris from a Public Dining Place in the Athenian Agora, Hesperia* Suppl. 25 (1992).

T. L. Shear Jr., The Persian Destruction of Athens: Evidence from Agora Deposits, in: *Hesperia* 62 (1993) 383–482.

E. Vanderpool, The Rectangular Rock-cut Shaft: The Shaft and Its Lower Fill, in: *Hesperia* 7 (1938) 363–411.

E. Vanderpool, The Rectangular Rock-cut Shaft: The Upper Fill, in: *Hesperia* 15 (1946) 265–336.

Ostraka from the Athenian Agora

A full catalogue and discussion of the Agora ostraka found before 1990 can be found in *Athenian Agora* XXV; Vanderpool 1973 also remains useful. The Kerameikos ostraka are discussed in detail in Brenne 2001. More about the operation of democratic government in the Agora can be found in Lang 2004 and Ober and Hedrick 1993.

Agora XXV = M. Lang, *Ostraka* (1990).

S. Brenne, *Ostrakismos und Prominenz in Athen: Attische Bürger des 5. Jhs. B.C. auf den Ostraka* (2001).

M. Lang, *The Athenian Citizen: Democracy in the Athenian Agora,* rev. by J. McK. Camp II, *Agora Picture Book* 4 (2004).

J. Ober / C. W. Hedrick, *The Birth of Democracy: Catalogue of an Exhibition Celebrating the 2500th Anniversary of Democracy at the National Archives, Washington, D.C.* (1993).

E. Vanderpool, Ostracism at Athens, in: *Lectures in Memory of Louise Taft Semple* (1973) 215–270.

A Pictorial History of the Agora Excavations

E. Antonatos / M. Mauzy, *Early Photographic Panoramas of Greece* (2003).

R. Burgess, *Greece and the Levant, or Diary of a Summer's Excursion in 1834, with Epistolary Supplements* (1835).

E. Chandler, *Photography in Ireland: The Nineteenth Century* (2001).

A. Delivorrias, *Athens 1839–1900: A Photographic Record* (1985).

E. Dodwell, *Views in Greece from Drawings by Edward Dodwell* (1821).

E. Dodwell, *Views and Descriptions of Cyclopean or Pelasgic Remains in Greece and Italy with Constructions of a Later Period, from Drawings by the Late Edward Dodwell* (1834).

R. Lenman, *The Oxford Companion to the Photograph* (2005).

C. L. Lyons / J. K. Papadopoulos / L. S. Stewart / A. Szegedy-Maszak, *Antiquity and Photography: Early Views of Ancient Mediterranean Sites* (2005).

C. A. Mauzy, *Agora Excavations 1931–2006: A Pictorial History* (2006).

A. Szegedy-Maszak, Félix Bonfils and the Traveler's Trail through Athens, in: *History of Photography* 25 (2001) 13–43.

A. X. Xanthakis, *History of Greek Photography: 1839–1960* (1988).

From Pot-Mending to Conservation: An Art Becomes a Science

A. Anastassiades / K. Abend / K. Lovén, On-site Storage of Metal Artifacts at the Athenian Agora, in: *Postprints of the Storage Symposium: Preservation and Access to Archaeological Materials June 6–8, 2008,* Cotsen Institute of Archaeology at UCLA (forthcoming).

C. Caple, *Conservation Skills: Judgement, Method, and Decision Making* (2000).

S. Gänsicke / P. Hatchfield / A. Hykin / M. Svoboda / C. M.-A. Tsu, The Ancient Egyptian Collection at the Museum of Fine Arts, Boston. Part I, A Review of Treatments in the Field and Their Consequences. Part 2, A Review of Former Treatments at the MFA and Their Consequences, in: *Journal of the American Institute for Conservation* 42 (2003) 167–236.

A. Oddy (ed.), *The Art of the Conservator* (1992).

J. K. Papadopoulos, *The Art of Antiquity: Piet de Jong and the Athenian Agora* (2007).

A. B. Paterakis, Conservation: Restoration versus Analysis? in: A. Roy / P. Smith (eds.), *Archaeological Conservation and Its Consequences: Preprints of the Contributions to the Copenhagen Congress, 26–30 August 1996* (1996) 143–148.

J. Unruh, Severely Degraded Textiles on Archaeological Artifacts at the Agora Excavations in Athens, Greece, in: J. L. Merrit / B. Halvorson / R. M. Hanson (eds.), *A Joint Session with the Objects Specialty Group Concerning Composite Objects, The Textile Specialty Group Postprints: Paper Delivered at the Textile Subgroup Session, American Institute for Conservation 30th Annual Meeting, Miami, Florida, June 2002,* Textile Specialty Group Volume 12, American Institute for Conservation, Washington, D.C. (2002).

Anchoring the Floating Monuments of the Agora

R. Anderson, Perspectives: Digital Graphics, in: *Journal of Field Archaeology* 29 (2004) 253.

D. Andrews / B. Blake / N. Fradgley / S. Lunnon / P. Roberts, *The Presentation of Historic Buildings Survey in CAD* (1999).

W. B. Dinsmoor Jr., The Archaeological Field Staff: The Architect, in: *Journal of Field Archaeology* 4 (1977) 309–328.

W. B. Dinsmoor Jr., Anchoring Two Floating Temples, in: *Hesperia* 51 (1982) 410–452.

Applying New Technologies

For more information about S 3497 and the recovery of the fragmentary grave stele see:

J. McK. Camp II, Excavations in the Athenian Agora, 2002–2007 in: *Hesperia* 76 (2006) 627–663.

CREDITS

Fig. 10: R. Townsend.

Fig. 78: J. Ober / C.W. Hedrick, *The Birth of Democracy: Catalogue of an Exhibition Celebrating the 2500th Anniversary of Democracy at the National Archives, Washington, D.C.* (1993).

Figs. 80, 83, 86: Gennadius Library Archives.

Fig. 81: National Historical Museum of Athens, Photographic Archive.

Fig. 82: Archaeological Society at Athens, Photographic Archive.

Fig. 84: German Archaeological Institute of Athens, Photographic Archive.

Fig. 89: Gernsheim Collection, Harry Ransom Humanities Research Center, University of Texas at Austin.

Fig. 91: Evi Antonatos Collection.

All other pictures from the authors / American School of Classical Studies at Athens.

ADDRESSES OF THE AUTHORS

John McK. Camp II
Craig A. Mauzy

Amandina Anastassiades
Richard C. Anderson
Bruce Hartzler

ASCSA, 54 Souidias St.
Athens 10676
Greece

Susan I. Rotroff
Washington University
Department of Classics
Campus Box 1050
1 Brookings Dr.
St. Louis, MO 63130
USA

Barbara Tsakirgis
Vanderbilt University
Department of Classical Studies
VU Station B #350132
Nashville, TN 37235
USA

Lee Ann Riccardi
College of New Jersey
Department of Art
PO Box 7718
Ewing, NJ 08628
USA

Mark L. Lawall
University of Manitoba
Department of Classics
366 University College
220 Dysart Rd.
Winnipeg, MB, R3T 2M8
Canada

Kathleen M. Lynch
University of Cincinnati
Department of Classics
410 Blegen Library
PO Box 210226
Cincinnati, OH 45221
USA

James P. Sickinger
Florida State University
Department of Classics
Tallahassee, FL 32306
USA

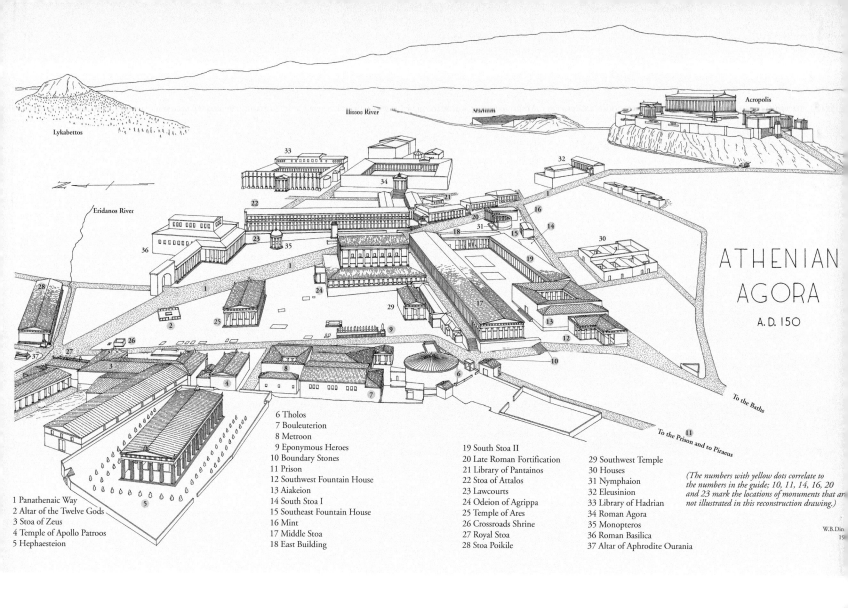

Lykabettos

Ilissos River

Stadium

Acropolis

Eridanos River

33

32

34

22

21

16

23

35

36

31

15

14

30

20

18

ATHENIAN
AGORA
A.D. 150

19

28

24

1

29

17

13

2

25

9

12

26

10

27

37

8

6

To the Baths

3

4

5

7

To the Prison and to Piraeus

11

1 Panathenaic Way
2 Altar of the Twelve Gods
3 Stoa of Zeus
4 Temple of Apollo Patroos
5 Hephaesteion

6 Tholos
7 Bouleuterion
8 Metroon
9 Eponymous Heroes
10 Boundary Stones
11 Prison
12 Southwest Fountain House
13 Aiakeion
14 South Stoa I
15 Southeast Fountain House
16 Mint
17 Middle Stoa
18 East Building

19 South Stoa II
20 Late Roman Fortification
21 Library of Pantainos
22 Stoa of Attalos
23 Lawcourts
24 Odeion of Agrippa
25 Temple of Ares
26 Crossroads Shrine
27 Royal Stoa
28 Stoa Poikile

29 Southwest Temple
30 Houses
31 Nymphaion
32 Eleusinion
33 Library of Hadrian
34 Roman Agora
35 Monopteros
36 Roman Basilica
37 Altar of Aphrodite Ourania

*(The numbers with yellow dots correlate to
the numbers in the guide; 10, 11, 14, 16, 20
and 23 mark the locations of monuments that are
not illustrated in this reconstruction drawing.)*

W.B.Din
19